The Six G.O.L.D. Keys to Well-Being

A Guide to Unlocking a Healthy and Happy Life

Welcome to the team, Monica!

xo
Alisha 5/6/22

Alisha Leytem

This book is dedicated to my husband, Michael,
and my daughter Melrose. I struck gold with you two.

Contents

The G.O.L.D. Method

"Yesterday I was clever, so I wanted to change the world.
Today I am wise, so I am changing myself."
– Rumi

In my heart, I always knew that I wanted to be an author someday. But my mind would always step in to remind me of why I wasn't ready, why I couldn't do it, and why it would never happen. For a long time, I listened to those thoughts. For a long time, I *believed* those thoughts.

When I made the conscious decision to shift my thoughts from why I couldn't into why I could, I found myself taking action. While I am very proud of myself for following through and writing this book, I am even more proud for changing the way I see myself. I chose to see myself as a published author. Whatever *your* dreams are, how might your life improve if you started to view yourself not as the person you can't become, but as the person you always knew you could be?

I believe one of the best questions we can ask is: *"Who am I and what do I want to become?"* The reason this is so powerful is because you are contemplating who you want to be instead of leaving it up to chance! Author Joe Dispenza says, *"The mere process of contemplating who you want to be begins to change your brain,"*[1] because changing your thoughts will change your life. When you are able to identify how you see yourself, you can then begin the process of seeing yourself in a new light.

This might feel overly simplified, but I promise you that this deep inner work of changing your mind is part of the lasting transformational process. Instead of seeing yourself as someone who is always "waiting" or "starting tomorrow," what if you started seeing yourself as the person who starts *right now*? If you see yourself as someone who doesn't have time to take care of yourself, then you will BE that person who doesn't have time to take care of themselves.

I deeply believe that the more happy people there are in the world, the better the world will become. Author Marianne Williamson says that "personal transformation can and does have global effects. As we go, so goes the world, for the world is us. The revolution that will save the world is ultimately a personal one."[2] I have found that the happier I become, the more I uplift others around me. Happy people create a ripple of joy — because when you work on changing and improving yourself, everyone around you benefits. This has become my mission: to create a ripple of change, *turning human beings into well-beings*.

My intention with this book is to offer you solutions through useful tools, transformational meditations, and mindful practices that will set you on a path of unlimited happiness and improved health. I am here to help you create lasting transformation.

The best way to get the results you desire from this book is to have an open mind and willingness to implement new habits and beliefs into your life. Big changes happen when you make little changes in your everyday habits. Know that growth is uncomfortable because it's unfamiliar, but this discomfort is exactly where growth happens.

After working with thousands of professionals through my wellness workshops, spiritual retreats, and corporate trainings, I've identified the six gold keys that make up a person's well-being. While these keys don't cover every single aspect of well-being, they provide a foundation for you to build upon. Use this book as an ongoing resource. Please don't feel like you have to use every piece of advice given — find what works for you and leave the rest.

The *secret* is to be open and remember that improving your well-being is a journey.

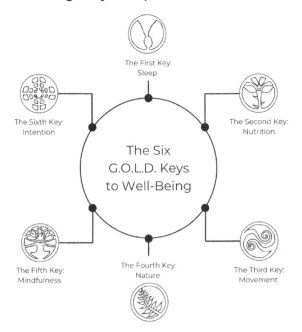

The First Key:
Sleep

The Sixth Key:
Intention

The Second Key:
Nutrition

The Six
G.O.L.D. Keys
to Well-Being

The Fifth Key:
Mindfulness

The Fourth Key:
Nature

The Third Key:
Movement

Where Should You Start?

The first option is to read this entire book from front to back and then choose which key you are going to focus on first based on your own intuition. You can't mess it up!

If you would like a little more direction, the second option is to take the *Six G.O.L.D. Keys to Well-being Assessment*, a five-minute online questionnaire that will email you a report with your results. This report will give you an overview of your current level of health and well-being, and offer insight into which key to start with! I highly recommend you complete this assessment and use your results as a guide throughout the book. You can take the free assessment at www.alishaleytem.com.

The results you receive from the assessment will give you deep insight into the thoughts that may run your life. Look at which of the six keys are your highest. How about the lowest? If, for example, your highest key is movement, — I would imagine that you see yourself as someone who exercises regularly and leads an active lifestyle. If, on the other hand, your lowest key is mindfulness, you might be seeing yourself as someone who is rushed and thinking about the past or future more than the current moment.

At the end of each chapter, you will find a summary of suggested actions and a list of affirmations to begin your personal transformation. Affirmations are positive statements that can help you challenge and overcome negative thoughts. When you repeat them often, you begin to believe them and find yourself making positive changes. Louise Hay, the queen of affirmations, teaches that "affirmations are like planting seeds in the ground. It takes some time to go from a seed to a full-grown plant. And so it is with affirmations — it takes time from the first declaration to the final demonstration. So, be patient."[3]

As you read the upcoming keys, reflect on these questions to see yourself in a new light:

- Who do I need to become in order to be the person who is _____ ? (e.g.: well rested, a healthy eater, active, grounded, living in the present moment, intentional, etc.)

- How will I integrate these keys and reinforce this new and different way of living?

- How can I continue to live these keys, day in and day out?

- What does it actually take to become a healthier and happier person — not just to know about it?

Whichever key you choose first, focus on implementing it for one to two weeks. Start slowly. Be gentle with yourself. Once you feel that the area has improved, trust yourself to move on to another key. This book isn't a race; remember that it's a journey. We want to create *lasting* transformation, which happens slowly.

I invite you to be radically honest with yourself as you read this book. If you find yourself feeling stuck, notice which of the six keys you are ignoring or perhaps resisting. The bigger the resistance the bigger the breakthrough, so I encourage you to lean into the key(s) that you feel the most resistance around, and watch how you uncover a new world of health and happiness.

Many people enjoy learning new information — it gives us a high! It's exciting to learn and it's invigorating to unlock wisdom. But eventually, the excitement wears off, and it becomes up to us to truly *integrate* what we have learned.

Integration is the **ultimate** key; reinforcing your new way of being is where you will find your biggest treasure and how you will shine the brightest! To help simplify this process of how to take the information and make real changes to transform your life, I created the G.O.L.D. Method.

The G.O.L.D. Method is a powerful journal technique designed to support you in finding a way forward on your journey. When you find that you are lacking power in an area of life, you can turn to the G.O.L.D. Method for an instant energetic shift. It is designed to help you identify what *is* and *is not* working for you, and then help you take what you are learning and do something differently.

I highly encourage you to take this journal prompt at the end of each key seriously. Resist the urge to skip this vital step when completing each chapter. You will get more out of this book and make the changes you deeply desire when you take the time to dig deep into this method. Consider keeping a journal or a document on your computer about what comes up for you with each of the prompts until you feel that you have embodied the shifts. Here's how it works.

The G.O.L.D. Method

Let's get started. You can answer the following prompts as they relate to each specific key, but also to anything else that is on your mind. The point is to consciously look at and process our thoughts, fears, and behaviors so that we can clear space to allow new energies to come in.

G is for Going Well

Start by reflecting on what *is* working for you, because no matter what you are experiencing in your life, something is always going well! When you choose to focus on what's going well, you are reinforcing all of the reasons that life is supporting you and that you are doing a good job. You are a whole and complete person *right now*. You are not broken and there is nothing for you to "fix."

Recognize that you are always doing the best you can, and so is everyone around you. Accept that you deserve good things – a good life, good relationships, good health and abundance. When you fully accept that you are worthy and deserving, you'll be amazed at how life flows and works for you! Let yourself acknowledge that even though you might not be exactly where you want to be, you are doing a good job and things are working out for you.

The well-being journey is about empowering yourself so that you can elevate your life.

Reflect on these prompts to help create clarity in your mind.

- When do I feel the most clear and connected?

- What is really working for me?

- Make a list of five things that are going well right now.

O is for <u>Obstacles</u>

Now that you've identified what's working, you can shift into listing what obstacles you are facing. If you ignore the fears or frustrations that are occurring for you, they tend to take up more space in your mind. Giving your fears or obstacles a voice helps you to take your power back. It helps you to identify any blocks that might be in the way and therefore gives them less importance.

It is especially important to remember that no matter how difficult they are, the obstacles are always things happening *for* us. When things happen for us, we learn the lessons that will guide us to the next level of whatever we are seeking (next-level happiness, next-level health, next-level peace, etc.)

This prompt is an opportunity to acknowledge what is getting in the way, so that then you can have more clarity about the things you can do differently.

- What stories or memories really bother me?

- What am I experiencing right now?

- What do I wish I could change?

- What makes me feel disempowered?

L is for <u>Learning</u>

What are you learning? There's power in reflecting on what you are learning and growing from with the current obstacles you are facing! This prompt helps to activate your "growth" mindset — the mind that is open to every possibility. The mind that is eager to learn knows that learning is how you become bigger and better.

When you seek to find the lessons in what you are experiencing, you are actively growing. Many people think that just because they are aging, they are growing. But time doesn't always mean growth.

Open your heart and reflect on what you are learning right now. This is to help you shift out of a "closed mindset" that life is happening *to* you and into the "growth mindset" that life is happening *for* you.

If you feel stuck on what you are learning, try asking yourself the following questions based on what you answered for the obstacles.

- What is this experience teaching me?

- What is something new or surprising that I have learned about myself?

- How can my present experience inform my future?

D is for <u>Do</u>

Now that you've identified what's working, what obstacles you're facing, and what you're learning — you have a better understanding of what exactly you can do differently moving forward. This is your opportunity to lean into the new version of you who welcomes growth! Change is not something that comes easily. Instead, change is something we must consciously dedicate our time and energy toward every day.

It requires the willingness to go where you haven't gone before. It's in the edges of discomfort that growth happens to transform your life. Your whole life can change a lot faster than you think. Commit to doing!

There's an energetic difference between saying you're going to do something and *deciding* you're going to do something. Deciding feels like a spark of hope that shakes your core.

Taking action by doing something means that you are leading yourself. Leading yourself means that you are in alignment with the best version of yourself, from moment to moment to moment. Dedicate yourself to living out your truest potential through your thoughts, actions, and way of being. Now ask yourself these questions:

- What do I need most *in this moment* to have my needs met?

- What am I going to *do differently* moving forward?

My intention is that by the end of this book, you will have increased confidence, real tools in your well-being toolbox, and a strong belief in yourself to create an even happier and healthier life!

Now that you are devoted to seeing yourself in a new light and you are equipped with a method to turn anything in your life into G.O.L.D., you are ready to unlock the six gold keys to well-being. At the end of the day, lead with these six keys and you will transform your health, life, and future into pure GOLD!

The Six
G.O.L.D. Keys

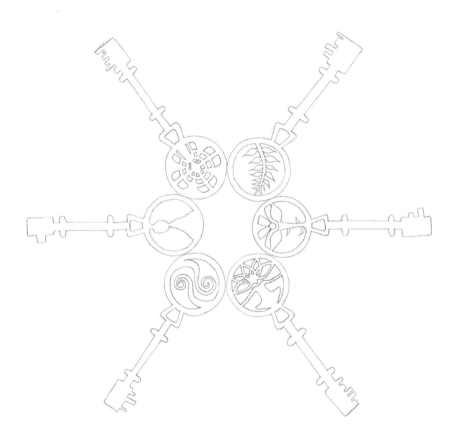

"Your life will be better if you're well rested.
Everything will be better if you're well rested."
– Kate Northrup

"The way to a more productive, more inspired,
more joyful life is getting enough sleep."
– Arianna Huffington

"Sleep is an investment in the energy you need
to be effective tomorrow."
– Tom Roth

CHAPTER 1

The First Key: Sleep

The gold key of sleep is the practice of relaxing the nervous system and naturally suspending consciousness to promote restoration.

Sleep is easily the most overlooked key to a person's well-being, yet it is essential for the body and mind to truly thrive. I deeply believe that we can change the world if more people engage in restful sleep night after night.

When you're tired from a lack of sleep, you aren't able to think clearly, show up in the way you want, or be truly healthy and happy. But when you *are* well rested, you are better able to meet your true self — the self who is kind, generous, non-judgmental, creative, and energized. When you sleep well at night, your body is rested and your mind is clear.

If you want to wake up feeling energized, well rested, and restored, the secret is how you *prepare* to have a great night of sleep. Most people don't think about what it means to actively let go of the day before going to sleep. You should be actively releasing the stresses of your day. So, while this key is ultimately about improving your sleep, my intention is to give you tools to let go of your stress from the day so that a deep, beautiful sleep is inevitable.

I take my sleep very seriously. I haven't always had this mindset, though! I used to equate sleep with increased anxiety. Sleep was something that I *had* to do. I would do everything I could to distract myself from going to sleep so that I could avoid the following day from coming (a common attitude sometimes referred to as the "Sunday Scaries"). I'd stay up late agonizing over the unpleasant events that happened in the day (a sign I was beating myself up). And I would stay up late purely for fun to do whatever I wanted to do (a sign of revenge bedtime procrastination).

When I started thinking about my sleep as a *non-negotiable* spiritual practice for my health and well-being, things changed. Now I sleep better, look forward to sleeping, and wake up feeling rested, renewed and excited for the day ahead.

I'm currently nursing my newborn as I begin writing this chapter. While the lack of sleep I'm getting right now is very real, I am grateful for what it reminds me about the healing power of sleep and how I've created a beautiful relationship with it over the years. I want to live in a world in which we share how much incredible sleep we are getting at night instead of how little. I desire us all to show off how great we are at taking care of ourselves!

Your Relationship with Sleep

Approximately one-third of all American adults don't get enough sleep. For some reason, people like to share about how little sleep they get at night as if it's a badge of honor. I would rather brag about how *much* sleep I get at night (ten hours of uninterrupted sleep is one of my favorite health magic tricks), but there's a deeper reason why we like to brag about how little sleep we get: we believe that our productivity is what makes us good enough or worthy.

If you tend to skimp out on sleep, or even talk about how little you get, reflect on what you believe it means to be well rested. Whenever I hear someone use their lack of sleep as a status symbol, I know that it is an opportunity for this person to cultivate true health and well-being. You do not have to sacrifice your health and well-being for productivity. You can be *both* a well-rested and productive person.

Rest Is Best

Start to look at your life in three areas: work, rest, and play. How much time do you spend at work? How much time do you spend resting? And how much time do you spend playing? Just like work and play, rest is absolutely essential to thriving! If you don't rest — and rest often — then your body will likely get sick and force you to rest anyway. You can be the person who is proactive and chooses to rest often, or you can be the person who doesn't rest until your body forces you to, the choice is yours. Thinking about relaxation in this way will hopefully help you see that rest is actually quite productive. Sleep is productive. When we sleep we are healing. We are getting out of activity mode and into rest mode. Repeat after me: Rest is best.

What Happens When We Don't Get Enough Sleep

Sleep is essential medicine and it impacts every single area of your well-being. When we don't get enough sleep, discomfort, disease, and disconnection can start to take over. Research shows that the time you spend sleeping is crucial to your health, brain function, and emotional well-being. Sleep influences everything from your weight to your emotions, to how you learn and process information, to your behavior and your productivity. Knowing this, isn't it wild that we don't prioritize deep sleep every single night?

While you are sleeping, your body is literally repairing itself. Your blood vessels are increasing and mending themselves, your immune system is strengthening, your hormones are balancing, and your skin is revitalizing itself, all as you sleep. So, what can happen when we don't get enough sleep?

Poor Mental and Emotional Health

Have you noticed how you lash out at others more easily when you're exhausted and low on sleep? Not only do our emotions go for a roller coaster ride when we're exhausted, but we are also at an increased risk of depression and anxiety.

Low Heart Health and Obesity

Research shows that chronic lack of sleep (defined as less than six hours per night) can endanger your heart health. According to the American Heart Association, an irregular sleep pattern is linked to obesity, high blood pressure, diabetes and heart disease.[4]

Increased Chances of Getting Sick

Chronic lack of sleep is proven to weaken your immune system. Saying no to that invite when you really feel like your body is asking for a solid ten hours of sleep can provide your immune system with just enough juice to prevent you from getting the bad cold that's going around.

Impulsive Decision-Making and Memory

The National Institute of Health published a study in 2000 that showed a significant lack of sleep can make you feel like you have a blood alcohol level (BAC) of 0.05 percent![5] This means sleepy decision-making can be just like making a decision when you've been drinking. Not only that, but when you sleep, your brain processes the day's events, which you need to have processed in order to have a brain that's ready for another day of making decisions and learning.

The Benefits of Getting Enough Sleep

Sleep Provides Solutions

The body works miraculously when you give it what it needs. When you get enough sleep at night, the body anchors in memories that you created that day and processes emotions. This is why we say "let me sleep on it" when we need to make a decision or get back to someone with a solution.

More Physical Energy and Creativity

When you're well rested, you have more energy to live your life. The more energized you are, the more you are able to access the creativity, solutions and ideas that are begging to be born through you.

Less Stress and Better Relationships

You aren't as emotionally reactive throughout the day when you get great sleep at night. This can improve all of your relationships from your home life to your work life.

Looking Your Best

There's a reason it's called "getting your beauty sleep." Your body is literally repairing itself while you sleep! This includes the appearance of your skin. Remember that when you feel good, you look good.

Increased Productivity

The irony of this is those who sacrifice their sleep for productivity have it backward: prioritize your sleep and you'll be even more productive the next day. Prioritizing sleep results in better focus, improved mood, and smarter decision-making, which all add up when you go to tackle your to-do list!

What About Naps?

A quick note on napping. For some reason, napping gets a bad rap in our culture. We see it as "lazy" and unproductive.

When done right, naps can help you reduce your fatigue, increase your focus, improve your mood, improve your performance, and help you to relax. It's time for us to change the story on naps and give it the credit it deserves. In fact, research has found that a daytime nap taken once or twice a week may lower the risk of having a heart attack![6]

The research on naps shows that power napping is more effective than long naps. A power nap is considered to be 15–20 minutes; anything longer than that can increase your risk of falling into a deep sleep. Long naps may be the culprit causing you to wake up groggy, or why you may have a hard time falling asleep later that night.

I've said this a million times before and will say it again throughout this book: *learn how to trust yourself.* Experiment with taking a fifteen-minute power nap in the middle of a workday and notice how you feel afterward. Did you feel refreshed? Rejuvenated? Or did you wake up feeling groggy and not able to fall asleep until later in the night?

Your body is always giving you messages about what it needs. If you're tired, stressed, and burnt out, listen to what it's trying to tell you and honor its needs. Your body is affecting your mind, and your mind is affecting your body. You function as a whole person. Honor this about yourself and be sure to listen to your body when it speaks!

Prioritizing Great Sleep Is a Radical Act of Self-Care

Why do we believe we have to give up taking great care of ourselves in order to thrive? Why do we believe that there is something superhuman about pushing through when you're exhausted and merely surviving the day? We have become so accustomed to living in a constant state of stress and lack of sleep that many people don't even realize this is something they can change. But know this: you hold the power to make the changes you desire in your life.

What would improve in your life if you became one of those people who made sleep their top priority? You can be well rested and still get everything done the next day. You can get plenty of sleep at night and still grow in your career. You can have a family and still prioritize great sleep. You are capable of feeling both truly rested and productive.

This doesn't mean that there won't be nights when the kids are keeping you up or traveling alters your sleep schedule, but the reality is that if you want to have a good relationship with sleep you need to make it a priority. You are becoming someone who takes great care of themselves by reading this book, so what steps can you take today to prioritize great sleep and keep that streak going?

10 Signs Your Sleep Routine Could Use an Upgrade

1. You are regularly waking up exhausted.

2. You suffer from insomnia and often wake up in the middle

of the night.

3. You grind your teeth and have scary dreams while you sleep.

4. You suffer from restless leg syndrome.

5. You have trouble falling asleep at night.

6. You consistently find yourself getting less than seven hours of sleep per night.

7. During the day, you experience brain fog and lack of focus.

8. You delay going to sleep *knowing* it will reduce your total amount of sleep time.

9. You stay up later than you intended to.

10. You don't have a regular time that you go to bed each night.

Why You Can't Sleep at Night

If you're struggling with getting great sleep at night, you aren't alone. Tens of millions of people experience a *chronic* lack of sleep, meaning their lack of sleep has been persisting for a long time. Researchers have found that many of the leading causes of sleepless nights are things within our control. The medicine of sleep can only truly restore us when we actively let go. This is about letting go of the day — the good and the bad — and simply sleeping. Ask yourself: are there any changes that I could make in my night routine that would help me fall and stay asleep more easily?

You Are on Your Phone Before Bed

Not only are screens keeping you up (and preventing your body's release of melatonin), but what you are consuming can have a harmful effect on your mind! Doomsday scrolling? Reading the news? Comparing yourself on social media? The final few minutes before you go to sleep are vital. Whatever you are watching or thinking about will imbed itself into your subconscious mind! All of this is triggering you and keeping you up later than you'd like.

You Don't Have a Routine

We easily give our children bedtime routines, yet when it comes to ourselves, we don't have one! If your child didn't have a routine to help anchor in sleepiness and time for bed, how would their sleep be at night? Same goes for you!

You Are Not Getting Enough Morning Sunlight

People who are exposed to morning sunlight tend to sleep better at night and are less depressed. Because we spend so much of our time indoors, we are losing our natural exposure to sunlight, which helps to balance our circadian rhythm, our natural internal clock. If you don't go outside in the morning and get exposure to the early sun, this will have an effect on your sleep.

You Don't Know How to Let Go of the Day

When you don't have the tools to manage your mental overload from the day, you end up carrying it with you to bed. Holding onto worry, resentment and concerns as you go into your bedroom sanctuary is preventing you from getting a great night of sleep. Decide to release your worries and concerns before bedtime. Choose to make your room a worry-free zone. Worry is simply a prayer for what we don't want, and this can keep us awake if our brain is buzzing with worry while we are trying to fall asleep. You must learn how to let go of the day and release what's heavy on your mind in order to successfully sleep at night.

You're Procrastinating for Revenge

Sleep revenge is a real issue, especially if you don't give yourself any personal time or self-care throughout the day. As a result, when it's time for sleep you might feel resentful that you didn't get any time to yourself, so you stay awake scrolling or doing whatever you'd like for "revenge."

You Don't Make It a Priority

This sounds like "I don't need sleep; I need to hustle and work." The more we understand our relationship with sleep and the thoughts we have about its importance, the better in touch with our own sleep habits we will become. This begs the question: where can I ask for more support during the day?

You Have Kids

Okay, there's not much you can do about this one. Just know

that this is temporary and this season will pass. But as a new mom who isn't getting as much great sleep as I did pre-baby, it's my duty to add this here. Tell yourself you are still getting great sleep — do *not* focus on the sleep you aren't getting as this will only make it worse. Acknowledgment and acceptance are key.

Ending the Sleep Revenge

The phenomenon of sleep revenge is happening more frequently because that time before going to sleep is likely the only time of the day that we feel we are getting to ourselves. Maybe you've spent all day helping others, working for others, taking care of others, and tending to our daily responsibilities, so you haven't had a minute to fill our own cup. Then...you procrastinate. You stay up late watching Netflix, YouTube, and Tik-Tok, knowing you are sabotaging your quantity of sleep, yet you can't help it. So, what should you do?

First: How can you ask for more help during the day so that you can find some time to fill up your own cup? Where can you say no? How can you accept the help and support that others are offering you?

Second: Be intentional with using the time you do have before bed to truly and fully fill up your own cup — physically, emotionally, and mentally. The more you engage in intentionally releasing the day, the more you are giving real, sustainable, beautiful energy back to yourself.

Mentally, this is about being able to positively review the day in our minds. When we replay the day and focus on everything good that happened, we can feel so much more fulfilled! I believe most people don't take the time to reflect on all of the magical things that happened, no matter how small, so they are constantly seeking out "more," when it's all already right there for you. Look for the *"Reflect on the Day to Put It Away"* exercise later in this chapter to help put this into practice.

Emotionally, the minutes before sleep are the time to really feel the beautiful moments of the day. Did you witness your child take her first step? Did you have a delicious dinner that you've been wanting to cook for a while? Did you nail that presentation at work and feel proud of yourself? This is what will truly give you the fulfillment you're seeking so that you willingly go to sleep and don't need any revenge! Are you holding onto the emotional turmoil of others that you were in contact with during the day? Your job is to understand that their emotions are not *yours*. In the words of Wayne Dyer, "You can't feel bad enough to make anyone else's life better."

Physically, it's about releasing the pent-up stress that was built up from the day's events. Being aware of how your body is feeling is important and knowing how to work with the body to release negative emotions is equally important. You can practice a relaxing, restorative yoga sequence by your bed. You can take a stress-relieving salt bath or a warm shower before hitting the sheets. This includes sex — having orgasms can release stress and help you to fall asleep more easily too.

Give to yourself what you are wanting from others. Do you want more support at work or at home? Allow yourself to be more supported in your thoughts by telling yourself what you would love to hear from others, such as, *You are doing a good job*. It's very important to accept compliments and not shrug them off or push them away.

If there's something that you want or need more of in your day in order to feel more satisfied, what can you do differently to get that need met? Stop allowing yourself to settle and refuse to not have your needs and desires met. Know that this is up to you. If this is an area that you are struggling with, later on, I will cover how to live your life with more intention in the sixth G.O.L.D. key to well-being. The more intentional and satisfied you are throughout your day, the easier this all becomes.

How to Create a Bedtime Routine

Imagine this scenario: You go to bed at night without bringing an ounce of stress with you. At the end of a long day you walk into your clean bedroom that is screen-free. Your space is filled with the aroma of diffused lavender and the low lighting of a salt lamp, a sound machine is lulling you to sleep, and an empty page in your journal is waiting for you to jot down what you're grateful for that day. You scan the previous twenty-four hours in your mind and are grateful for the magical moments and the lessons learned. You easily fall asleep with meditation and wake up the next morning feeling well rested and reju-venated after a solid eight hours of deep, quality sleep. The temperature of the room was perfect throughout the night, and you awoke feeling energized and ready for a beautiful day ahead.

If this isn't how a typical night of sleep is for you, it's time we change that — and since you're reading this book, trust that you are ready and able to do so.

Before you can create a beautiful sleep routine that works for you, you have to start by looking at your current relationship with sleep: your patterns, habits, and behaviors that are all driving your current sleep schedule. Begin by grabbing your journal and reflecting on the following questions:

- How many hours of sleep are you getting, on average, per night?

- What time do you typically go to sleep?

- What do you do before going to sleep? (What are you watching, reading, and thinking?)

- What time do you typically wake up?

- Of those hours in bed, how many of them are spent in deep sleep?

- How many hours per night are you awake, tossing and turning?

- On the nights that you weren't able to sleep very well, what happened the day prior? What did you do (or not do) to release and let the day go beforehand?

I recommend taking a week to track these patterns to give you a better idea of where you are currently, so we can find what works best for you. Even more important is your understanding of your body's sleep needs. Some people require nine hours each night, while others do great with seven hours. What's most important is that you find what your magic number is.

Refer to this chart throughout the week to help you identify what is or is not working for you right now.

Day of Week	Time to Bed	Time to Wake	What You Did Before Going to Bed	How Rested You Feel in the Morning
Sunday				
Monday				
Tuesday				
Wednesday				
Thursday				
Friday				
Saturday				

Once you've tracked your sleep for a solid week, make a note of all of the habits that aren't supporting you. The more honest you are with yourself in this process, the better results you'll have. No judgment allowed here, just pure honesty and curiosity.

Dedicate Yourself to New Bedtime Habits

For each habit you've identified that isn't serving you, you can focus on replacing that habit with something that will. Studies show it's easier to add something in than it is to remove something when it comes to behavior change!

For example, maybe you notice that you often have a late-afternoon coffee to get you through the rest of the day, but then you have a hard time falling asleep at night. What you might choose to do moving forward is replace that late-day coffee with an herbal tea instead of saying "no more afternoon coffee."

Or maybe you realize that you are doing the "sleep revenge" thing, and to overcome that, you design a bedtime routine you look forward to that truly fills up your cup after a long day, such as taking a hot bath or reading an enjoyable book that you look forward to.

Perhaps you're realizing that you are thinking thoughts that aren't helping you such as "I'm not a good sleeper." Now you can decide to work on changing this thought pattern with a new affirmation: "I choose to believe sleep comes easily to me".

Real Tools for Better Sleep

Now that you've done an honest inventory of your sleep patterns, habits and beliefs, let's continue to cover some practical tools that will assist you in getting better sleep.

Better sleep happens when you process and release the day to prepare your mind and body for rest and relaxation. Your body needs to shift into sleep mode. Here are some of my favorite practical tools to help you do so:

Living Areas

- Lower the lights in your home to prepare for sleep. Turn off as many lights as you can as soon as the sun goes down (this will help to align your circadian rhythm). Consider using candle light or pink himalayan salt lamps for the rest of the evening. Bonus points for the coziness!

- Take fifteen minutes to tidy up your kitchen, living room, and bedroom. Research has shown that having a clean, organized home can help you sleep better!

- Turn on relaxing and calming music throughout your home.

Lifestyle

- 3-2-1 Sleep: 3 hours before bed, no food or alcohol. 2 hours before, no work. 1 hour before, no screens.

- Stop working (including answering emails and texts) at

least two hours before going to sleep. Because many can now work from anywhere, it's hard to truly go offline. Honoring your sleep means you have to set a hard boundary with yourself (and others) for what time you stop working at night.

- Turn off the screens one hour before bed. Exposure to light controls your circadian rhythm, or your natural sleep-and-wake cycle. Blue light from electronics blocks your hormone called melatonin, which we need enough of to help us become sleepy. If you must use screens, consider wearing blue-light eyeglasses so that your body will still increase its melatonin naturally.

- Give yourself a bedtime and stick to it (aim to be in bed no later than 10:00 p.m. because sleeping during 10 p.m.–2 a.m. is best for your nervous system).

- Refrain from caffeine after 2:00 p.m. — research has shown that caffeine after 2:00 p.m. can have a negative effect on some people's ability to sleep at night.

- Try to go to sleep within the same hour every night (including weekends).

Mind

- Listen to guided meditations that help you relax and gently lure you to sleep.

- Journal to release the day. Write out what you're grateful for, and list anything else that is on your mind so that it's out of your head and onto the paper.

- Visualize yourself doing something well. Visualization is scientifically proven to help you fall asleep faster.[7] Visualize yourself in a peaceful place like a beach, or picturing yourself doing something that you are good at (maybe this is cooking your favorite meal or fishing).

- Read a chapter from a light book. (Refrain from reading heavy material before bed! For example, if you're struggling with parenting, reading a parenting book might cause you stress and be a little too heavy as you fall asleep — stick to light material that makes you feel good.)

- Pray and read a spiritual text that resonates with you.

Bedroom

- No TV in the bedroom — a bedroom should be for sleep and sex only.

- Regulate your room's temperature — research has shown that bedrooms kept at 65 degrees Fahrenheit aid with falling and staying asleep. You can play with this number and see what works best for you!

- Consider sleeping with a sound machine. Using the same sound before bed can remind your body that it is time to "turn off" and prepare for sleep.

- Use aromatherapy. (We'll deep dive into how to use essential oils to aid with sleep in the coming pages).

Bedding

- Use a weighted blanket.

- Invest in organic, high thread count sheets and wash them at least 1–2 times per week.

- Use quality pillows (replace them often).

- Invest in a quality mattress. You spend a lot of your life in bed, so consider purchasing a non-toxic mattress to limit your exposure to toxic pesticides, chemical dyes and other treatments.

Body

- Practice relaxing yoga poses before bed.

- Take a detox salt bath by soaking for 20–30 minutes in the tub with 1 cup of unscented Epsom salts.

Relaxing Bedtime Yoga Routine

I've been teaching yoga for years, and as a result I see all the time how powerful a relaxation yoga sequence can be for everyone. I can feel the heavy, stressful energy that is held by students when they enter the class and how much of that has been lifted when they leave. There's a reason that yoga feels so good, and it's because of the insane effect it has on your mind and body. It's not just wishful thinking either — a national survey found that over 55 percent of people who did yoga found that it helped them get better sleep. Over 85 percent said yoga helped reduce stress.[8] And yes, it's for every *body*.

Here is a simple yoga routine that I've designed specifically for you to let go of the day's stresses and connect with your body. You can do it for as little as five minutes before bed. These poses are gentle and easily accessible, so if you are brand-new to yoga, please do not be intimidated!

Aim to spend at least one solid minute per pose and up to five minutes in each pose. You can start at twenty seconds and work your way up. Your breath is vital to be able to relax in these poses; be conscious of breathing deeply and fully for each breath. If you'd like more guidance on how to breathe deeply, refer to the upcoming chapter about the key of mindfulness.

Child's Pose

Bring your big toes together underneath you and spread your knees out wide. Walk your hands forward as far as you can and then gently lay your forehead down on the mat or bed so that your heart is softening into the ground. Make sure your sit bones are rested on your heels, and feel free to add a pillow above your heels if your sit bones do not reach. You can rest your forehead on a yoga block or stack several pillows underneath your head to bring the ground closer to you. Take five deep and relaxing gentle breaths.

Seated Forward Fold

Sitting down with your legs straight out in front of you, bring your arms straight up into the sky with a straight back. Take a deep breath in, and as you exhale, allow your upper body to "fold" over your legs. Let your hands rest on the ground wherever is most comfortable to you. You can place a pillow on top of your legs in order to bring the ground closer to you. Take five cleansing breaths as you hold this position.

Supine Twist

Lying on your back with your legs straight and out, bring your left knee into your chest and hug it with your hands. Keep your right hand on your left knee, and bring your left arm out to a T with the palm facing down. Use your right hand as you exhale to guide the left knee across your body for a gentle twist. Bring your gaze to look over at your left palm to gently deepen the twist. Stay for five cleansing breaths. Switch sides and repeat.

Legs Up the Wall

Find an empty wall. Bring your yoga mat or a blanket next to the wall. Sit sideways with the wall at your arm and turn gently to lie on your back as you bring your legs to rest on the wall. If you are doing this sequence in your bed, feel free to use your bed frame as your wall. The bottoms of your feet should be facing up toward the ceiling, and keep your bottom as close to the wall as possible. Keep a slight bend in your knees. Your hands can be down by your sides, palms facing up, or they can rest on your stomach. You can stay here for up to twenty minutes — this is an epic pose to increase blood flow and release stress from the mind and body prior to sleeping.

You can also do this pose anytime during the day when you are feeling tired. It is said that twenty minutes in this pose can feel like a two-hour nap.

Supported Bridge Pose

Begin lying on your back with your knees bent

at 45-degree angles and your feet pressing into the ground, hip-width distance apart. Using a yoga block or pillow, gently lift your hips off of the ground and place the prop underneath the small of your back. Carefully set your hips back onto the prop. Stay in this pose for at least twenty seconds and allow the stress to release from your body.

Savasana

This final pose is very important, yet it is one that many like to skip. It looks as though you're doing "nothing," but remember that rest is the most productive thing we can do. Resting *is* doing something. To do this final pose, simply lie on your back. Let your arms rest out by your hips with your palms facing up toward the sky and several inches away from your body (you will naturally feel your chest opening up and your shoulder blades pressing into the ground). Allow your legs to be straight with your feet just over hip-width distance. Close your eyes and allow the energies you've cleansed to settle throughout your body as you simply relax and get out of the way. Stay here for several minutes, or if you are in your bed, allow yourself to drift off to a magical sleep.

Aromatherapy for Sleep

Aromatherapy is an incredible tool for helping you fall and stay asleep. Aromatherapy works because when you breathe in an oil, you are activating the brain through your sense of smell. Diffusing high-quality essential oils (please note that there is a difference between high-quality essential oils and perfume-like scents) supports optimal and restful sleep because breathing in the oils relaxes tense muscles and calms active minds. Diffusing calming essential oils in your room at night helps your mind to relax and signals your brain to begin unwinding.

I recommend turning on an essential oil diffuser placed on your nightstand ideally thirty minutes before you go to sleep. When you are ready to go into your bedroom, the space will be ready for you as a beautiful wellness sanctuary filled with gorgeous aromas that will support you in relaxing.

Essential Oil Diffuser Blends For Sleep

CEDAR SLEEP:
4 drops Cedarwood
2 drops Lavender

WELLNESS SANCTUARY:
2 drops Lavender
2 drops Orange

LET THE DAY GO:
2 drops Lavender
2 drops Vetiver
2 drops Marjoram

RELAX AND GROUND:
4 drops Frankincense
2 drops Vetiver

Apply Essential Oils on Bottoms of Feet

You can also apply essential oils to the bottoms of your feet to promote relaxation and sleep. The bottom of your feet have very large pores, so applying pure plants in the form of essential oils onto your feet is a quick way for the plants to access your bloodstream quickly. Simply apply 1–2 drops of an essential oil on the bottoms of your feet and then use your hand to rub it in. My favorite essential oils to apply topically to support restful sleep are vetiver, juniper berry (known to help with nightmares), lavender, cedarwood, and roman chamomile.

Natural Sleep Supplements

Sometimes we need a little more help to combat high levels of stress and insomnia. If you choose to try any of these natural supplements to help you wind down at night, it's best to do so between thirty minutes and an hour before your bedtime. This gives the compounds time to calm and ease your mind before you start trying to fall asleep.

Chamomile – Drink a cup of warm, organic chamomile tea before going to sleep.[9]

Cherry juice – Drink one tablespoon of tart, organic cherry juice at night. Studies show that this may help with insomnia, improve melatonin levels, and reduce inflammation to promote better sleep.[10]

Magnesium Glycinate – Magnesium deficiencies can disrupt your sleep cycle. Magnesium glycinate promotes healthy sleep patterns and improves sleep quality. Studies suggest taking 300–400 milligrams per day and you can get it at a health-food store, or online.

Lavender – Drink as a tea, use as a bed-sheet spray, or apply a high-quality oil directly to your feet (lavender contains high amounts of L-theanine, which supports relaxation).

Journal Prompts for Better, Deeper Sleep

The following journal prompts will help you raise your emotional state before bed (the emotion you feel when you fall asleep will typically be how you feel when you're awake).

- What were three great things that happened today?

- What three things am I ready and willing to let go of today? List them out by completing this sentence: I choose to let go of _____ with ease and grace.

- Finish this sentence and repeat it ten times total: I am grateful for _____, because _____.

- Free write: What is weighing heavy on my mind that I would like to release prior to sleeping? (Remember that when you put your thoughts to paper, it gives your mind a break from holding onto the thought!)

- What am I looking forward to experiencing tomorrow?

- Write down your favorite bedtime affirmations (refer to the end of this chapter for a list of affirmations to support your sleep).

Mindfulness Exercise: *Reflect on the Day to Put It Away*

Reviewing our day means to mentally go over the events of the past twenty-four hours with an open and non-judgmental mind. When we review the day we just had, we can better notice the moments we were patient and the moments we were not. We typically remember things we forgot happened. This exercise keeps us in a growth mindset. Here's how to do it.

Keep a journal and pen nearby, close your eyes, and sit or lie in a comfortable position. Begin to mentally scan the day that you just experienced, starting with looking at our day with gratitude. As the Dalai Lama says, we are fortunate to be alive, and we must be grateful for this blessing.

Review your past twenty-four hours by remembering all of the events that occurred. See yourself as you went about your day, being aware of both the good moments and the not-so-good moments. When you come upon a great moment, let yourself relive that moment again! (This is a powerful tool for feeling good). When you come upon a moment that wasn't so great, pause and self-reflect: Why did I do this? What was I thinking at that moment? What could I have done differently? Looking at the emotional details helps you to stop repeating the same habits that hinder you and continue making the choices that support you. Instead of beating yourself up or being hard on yourself for what happened, forgive yourself and vow to make a different choice next time you are faced with a similar situation.

Once you finish reviewing your day, say thank you. Thank you for all of the beautiful moments and lessons learned. Thank you for showing me when I was at my best and for showing me when I was not.

Set an intention for tomorrow: *Tomorrow, I intend to be more aware, be kind to myself, and be happy.*

To complete this exercise, write down in your journal all of the moments you remembered that you are grateful for. What you focus on grows, and the more we focus on what we are grateful for, the more we will have to be grateful for! Once you close your journal for the night, make a mental note that *the day is done, I have done my best. I let go of the rest and now it's time for rest. I choose to release the day. It is time for sleep now. I am worthy of getting a great night of sleep. It feels so good to prioritize my sleep. I enjoy preparing my mind and body for deep rest. Just for tonight, no matter what is happening in my life, I choose to set it down and let myself sleep.*

Meditations for Better Sleep

The Dalai Lama says that "sleep is the best meditation." Refer to these guided meditations to help you relax, fall and stay asleep. You can get into bed and ask a partner to read the script out loud to you, record yourself on your phone to listen or you can listen to these guided meditations at www.alishaleytem.com.

A Meditation for Evening Gratitude

The day is now done and the experiences are over. It is now time to let the day go. Let the work stay where the work belongs. Whether you had the best or worst day — it is over. So, let it go.

With ease and love, turn your attention to this very moment. This is the only moment that is real. This moment is a time for relaxing, letting go and preparing ourselves for sleep.

Sleep is a time when we restore and repair ourselves. Our minds move into a state where problems of the day are solved and we prepare for the new day. When we go to sleep, we are wrapping up the day and preparing ourselves for a new day.

Let the body relax, and become very, very comfortable.

Take a nice deep breath and let go.

Relax your head. Relax your belly. Relax your legs. It feels so good to close your eyes and relax.

Feel your entire body relax. Allow every cell in your body to relax.

Give your emotions permission to simply let go.

Feel the peace in your mind and body.

We want to take positive thoughts with us when we go to sleep. So, if there's any anger, resentment, or rage — let it go. If there's any fear or worry — let it go. Any negative emotion that is lingering in your mind — let it go.

Release the need to be critical or judgmental of yourself or others. Be willing to accept and approve of yourself and others.

In this very relaxed state, reflect on all the things you're grateful for: loved ones, fresh air in your lungs, the food in your fridge, and your comfortable home.

As you think about what you're grateful for, visualize yourself saying "thank you" to each thing.

Let yourself imagine and feel it as much as you can.

Let the feeling of gratitude for these things beam out from your heart.

Let a smile wash over your face as you relax into gratitude.

If you're having a hard time coming up with things to be grateful for, say a prayer to your higher power to show you images and reveal to you what you can give thanks to in your life.

Allow the feeling of deep gratitude to come into your body.

Notice where the feeling lives.

Let this feeling spread out into every cell in your body.

Thank you, thank you, thank you.

Allow this feeling of gratitude to wash away any negativity or tension from the day.

Feel into this deep state of gratitude and relaxation.

Bring this feeling of gratitude with you as you allow yourself to fall into a beautiful sleep.

Yoga Nidra Guided Meditation for Deep Relaxation

This guided yoga nidra meditation will support you in whatever position you find yourself comfortable in. This will be a friend to your rest, relaxation, and sleep rhythms. Sleep is so essential, and when we can't sleep, it can be due to physical, mental, and emotional factors — or a combination of all three. Yoga nidra offers us tools to induce sleep organically following your own mind.

Allow yourself to become as comfortable as possible. Notice your senses — listen with your ears and whole body, feel the support of the ground under your body, feel the air touching your nose, and notice the darkness and stillness with your eyes closed.

Now, set your intention for this practice. Ask yourself in your life right now, what is your deepest most heartfelt desire? Think of this as a little seed that you're planting into your time in the world of sleep — like a blessing that you sprinkle through your sleep.

As you think about this intention, see and FEEL your life with the fulfillment of this desire. What would your life look, sound, smell, taste, and feel like if this deepest desire were a reality?

Allow your attention to be on your breath without controlling it. As you relax into the simplicity of breathing...simply breathe. Notice how your body spreads like water. Feel how within this body of water, there is a rhythm, a tide. Waves of breath, ebbing and flowing. Feel how awareness of the tide of your breathing can deepen awareness of the flow of all life. See and feel how the simple process of releasing and welcoming the quiet breath is mirrored in the flow of the day in your life. As day flows into night and night flows into day. As winter flows into summer and summer flows into winter.

Now begin to count backward on each exhale, starting from ten, until you reach zero. Listen to the sound of my voice.

Inhale, Exhale (Ten), Inhale, Exhale (nine), Inhale, Exhale (eight), Inhale, Exhale (seven), Inhale, Exhale (six), Inhale, Exhale (five), Inhale, Exhale (four), Inhale, Exhale (three), Inhale, Exhale (two), Inhale, Exhale (one), Inhale, Exhale (zero).

Now bring your awareness to the tongue in your mouth, jaws, gums, teeth, lips. The entire mouth. Cheeks and cheekbones, chin, forehead, ears, earlobe, nose, and tip of nose. Both nostrils. Both eyes and the space just underneath the eyes. Full of awareness. Both eyebrows and the space between the eyebrows. Temples. Top of the head. Back of the head. Back of the neck. The whole head as one sensation.

Feel both shoulders. The upper arms. The elbows. Forearms. Wrists. Palms of the hands, backs of the hands. Thumbs, second fingers, third fingers, fourth fingers, pinky fingers. Feel the spaces between the fingers, the tips of the fingers, each finger like a little stream that flows into the space beyond. Now feel the chest and the upper back. Feel the ribcage and the middle back. Feel the belly and the low back. The pelvis, and the butt. Both hips, sensation in the thighs, knees, and the space just underneath the knees. Lower legs, ankles, heels, soles of the feet, tops of the feet, big toe, second toe, third toe, fourth toe, pinky toe. Feel the spaces between the toes. The tips of the toes. Each toe like a stream that flows into the space beyond. Feel the whole body at once. Each individual sensation, melting into a mass of relaxation.

Be aware of the whole body — from the top of your head to the bottom of your heels.

Let yourself relax even deeper. Feel the skin. Go beneath the skin and feel the tissues and muscles and deeper still to feel the muscles and let the muscles rest, deeply.

Go even deeper into relaxation — go into your bones and the layers within the bones, as though the bones themselves can relax on command.

Becoming deeper and deeper, relaxed and sleepy.

The heartbeat is slowing down. All the organs in your body committed to deep relaxation and rest.

Feel the fluids in the body and the cells humming as one — committing to deeper relaxation. Can you go even deeper into relaxation?

Now bring your attention to a sensation of heaviness. Welcoming the sensation of heaviness in some or all parts of the body. Now bring your attention to a sensation of lightness in some of all parts of the body.

Give yourself up to heaviness. Relax into heaviness. Go back to *the sensation of lightness. Give yourself up to lightness. Relax into lightness.*

Back into the sensation of heaviness — arms and legs heavy. Head and belly heavy. Back to the sensation of lightness — arms and legs light and weightless. Head and belly light and floating. Feeling so light.

Now feel both simultaneously — heavy and light at the same time. Don't try to think about this — just feel. Heaviness and lightness.

Now notice, what is your experience with your body right now? Let your body answer the question. Set your attention free to a feeling of just being. Nothing to do. Nothing to know or get or want.

Let go completely of time and space. Notice what is left. Let yourself fall into the heart space and empty the mind completely of any images, thoughts, stories, or feelings. Empty totally and completely into the heart space, allowing yourself to become even more deeply rested.

A Summary of How to Unlock the Gold Key of Sleep

1. Begin seeing sleep as an essential practice for your body and mind to truly thrive.

2. Prioritize preparing for sleep by intentionally letting go of everything that happened in the day.

3. Try aromatherapy, guided meditations, journaling, yoga poses, and supplements to help you fall asleep with ease.

4. Design your own night time routine to prepare your mind, body, and spirit for sleep.

5. Practice the *Reflect on the Day to Put It Away* Mindfulness Exercise.

Affirmations for The Gold Key Of Sleep

- I am grateful for today and now rest easy.

- I sleep easily and peacefully.

- The day is over; I have done my best and I let go of the rest.

- My bedroom is relaxing, and I easily fall asleep now, without guilt and with deep gratitude.

- I choose to believe that sleep comes easily to me.

- I have a bedtime routine that I enjoy and look forward to every night.

- I honor my needs and am deserving of restful sleep.

- I easily release the day from my mind and prepare for great sleep at night.

- I am learning. I am growing. I am excited for tomorrow. I believe in me.

Turn Your Sleep into G.O.L.D.

Grab your journal and use these prompts to reflect on your next steps for unlocking this key:

G: What's **going well** with your sleep?

_____

_____

_____

_____

O: What **obstacles** are you facing with your sleep?

_____

_____

_____

_____

L: What are you **learning** about your relationship with sleep from this chapter?

_____

_____

_____

_____

D: What will you **do** to improve your sleep moving forward?

_____

_____

_____

_____

Do not underestimate the power of sleep for your overall well-being. It may be simple, but it has a lot of power in what it has to offer you! In the next chapter, you will learn how to improve your nutrition by getting to the basics of food, cooking, and where your health really begins — in the gut!

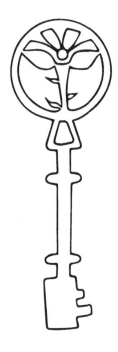

"*Good nutrition creates health in all areas of our existence.*
All parts are interconnected."
– T. Collin Campbell

"*A healthy outside starts from the inside*"
– Robert Urich

CHAPTER 2

The Second Key: Nutrition

The gold key of nutrition is the practice of consuming the nourishment required for optimal health and well-being.

Proper nutrition is vital to your health and well-being, because food drives the chemistry in your body. You become what you eat. In this chapter, I am going to help you understand the power of nutrition, how to eat in season, and the link between a healthy gut and a healthy mind.

We all know that eating healthy is one of the best and fastest ways to improve your overall health. However, why don't more people do it? It's estimated that by 2030, close to half of the US population will be obese.[11] And the lack of nutrition is rubbing off on our children, because they are becoming more obese at an alarmingly fast rate, with a study finding that the percentage of obesity in children and teens grew to 22 percent during the pandemic![12]

We've become a culture of convenience, particularly with our food. We have been sold and advertised to purchase "food" that is ready-made and processed beyond recognition. We've lost the art of home cooking and have fallen prey to what we think is "cooking" — opening up a package of prepared food and reheating it.

We have filled our lives with so much activity, work, and scrolling that we have lost the importance of being truly connected to our food, *real* food. We are disconnected from where it came from, how it came to our table, who grew it, and if it gave its life up for us. (Wait...there's more to a chicken than just the breast?)

This bad habit of convenience with food really started in the 1950s, when the frozen TV dinner was invented. We've been taught that cooking takes way too much time and that it isn't worth the effort. What's interesting is that when we learn how to cook and prepare simple meals for ourselves with real food, it's actually much faster than the "fast food" we've been taught to purchase! (More on that later in this chapter.)

But why does this matter? How is improving your diet benefiting you? There are countless reasons to eat healthier, but just to name a few, eating real foods and home-cooked meals will: improve your heart health, prevent diseases, increase your energy levels, make you smarter, support your mental health, help you sleep better, improve your immune system, and nourish your overall mood. The way I see it, if you start eating better, you can change your entire life — everything from your mental health to your vitality!

Like many others, I grew up eating meals that were processed and primarily premade. I wasn't interested in vegetables because I had no real connection to where they came from and why I needed them. When someone ordered a pizza in my college dorm building, people assumed that I had ordered it (I usually did), and every trip to my college cafeteria wasn't complete without several plates of fried food. I had no idea what real food was. I thought if I could consume it, it was "real food."

It wasn't until I accepted a part-time job working the table at a weekly farmers' market that I reached a turning point. Suddenly, I was surrounded by tables and tables of local fruits, vegetables, and herbs that I had literally never seen before in my life. I was so intrigued watching people purchase produce directly from the farmers who had grown it themselves. I remember feeling so alive simply by being in the presence of the living food — food that was grown within a short radius from where we were! For the first time in my life, I was able to see firsthand the people who were growing real food right in my backyard.

I started purchasing some vegetables when I finished my shift and immediately went home to try cooking them. I noticed that the entire process — learning about the food from the farmers, cooking and preparing it myself, and eating it — was improving my overall well-being. I was developing a deep connection with the food, since I knew where it was grown and the people who had grown it. It was like a new world to me, and it made me feel so alive. I was discovering the simplicity in cooking fresh foods and it was adding joy to my life — not removing it!

Working at the farmers' market made me understand that my disconnection from real food was creating a focus on eating for taste and convenience, rather than for my health. While I believe in eating for taste and convenience (I consider myself a true foodie), it's vital that we aim for the majority of our meals to be dense with nutrients! We can and we *must* view food as nourishment not only for our bodies, but for our mind and souls.

Working the information desk at the farmers' market that one summer truly sparked my healthy living journey. I spent the following years studying and learning about nutrition. I devoured nutrition books and blogs, listened to hundreds of hours of nutrition podcasts, attended nutrition classes, and watched cooking shows to teach myself how to cook.

What I've learned is that there is a simple solution to better nutrition: the closer we eat to nature, the closer we are to optimal health. The more alive foods we eat, the more alive we feel. But where to begin? Sometimes it's helpful to look at where the gaps are in your everyday diet and build on it from there.

Common Nutritional Gaps

Just because something is common doesn't mean that it's normal or healthy. Notice which of these gaps (if any) you find yourself doing on the daily. This activity isn't about judging yourself; it's about bringing more awareness so that you can make the changes needed to move forward.

- *Your diet is overloaded with sugar, salt, unhealthy fats, and*

processed foods, all of which have properties that nega-
tively impact the body and cause serious damage when
eaten frequently.

- *You don't eat enough healthy fats.* The fat-phobia of the
eighties and nineties was really why people in our society
are still afraid of fats. Please don't fear *healthy* fats; they
are the sources of essential nutrients we need to function.
Your brain is made up of healthy fat, so eating healthy
fat means you are supporting a healthy brain. I will share
more about what exactly a healthy fat is later.

- *You consume more sodium than is recommended.* Excessive
amounts can lead to serious cardiovascular problems, and
every food item you open from a package is loaded with
sodium.

- *You don't eat enough veggies each day,* which creates an
overall lower quality of life. You have to be really intentional
about eating enough veggies each day to get them in! I
will share some tricks for how to do this to make it easier for
you. This is important because veggies keep our immune
systems strong and allow our bodies to have higher
amounts of energy and better digestion.

- *You don't drink enough water,* yet you drink plenty of everything else: soda, fruit juices, energy drinks, sugar-loaded
coffees. If you simply replaced these drinks with water, you
would exponentially increase your energy levels simply by
being properly hydrated.

For some reason, healthy eating has become complicated here in the West. We are confused about what to eat. Do we focus on calories or ingredients? Macros or micros? Vegan or meat heavy? Lots of carbs or carb free? The question then is, with all of the information on food and different diets out there, *how do we know what to actually eat?*

Are You Eating Real Food?

Every cell in your body is made up of what you eat. If you are consuming artificial, packaged products, chances are that your body and mind will not be in an optimal state of health. When you eat foods as nature intended, your body will recognize these foods and send them to all the right places.

In the groundbreaking book *Food Rules,* author Michael Pollan sums up what it means to eat real food in three parts: *"Eat Food. Not Too Much. Mostly Plants."* One of my favorite tips he gives in his book is: "Don't eat anything your great-grandmother wouldn't recognize as food."[13]

How do we define what real food is? *Real foods are foods that are as close to their natural state as possible.* Meaning, you could go straight to the earth and get it yourself. It doesn't require going through a factory to be processed into something else entirely. For example, an organic chicken thigh is real food; an Impossible Burger patty is not real food. Meat is not the enemy; engineering ourselves away from nature is. If it doesn't come in a box and it hasn't been preserved, it's real food (unless you did it yourself and like to preserve your own food!).

Another way to think of this is to eat the rainbow. It's recommended to consume at least five servings of veggies and fruits each day. Try not to let this overwhelm you. If you focus on adding more veggies into what you are currently consuming (i.e. eat your pasta over a bed of greens), then you will more easily hit this mark each day. It doesn't have to become a big deal; it just has to become a natural part of who you are and the small everyday habits you choose.

When you focus on eating real foods, you are staying as close as possible to their natural, high-vibration energetic state. This helps you to feel full and nourished, eat less, and lose weight without feeling like you're on a diet. Your mood is better. Your energy improves. Your skin is more clear. Your life is better. Your well-being improves. Here are more examples of what real food is and is not:

The Modern Diet (not real food)

- Genetically modified (GMO) food, and conventional food that's been treated with chemicals and pesticides

- Low fat foods

- Refined salt and refined sugars

- Sodas and other artificially flavored drinks

- Conventional meat or animals from cages

- Processed, packaged, canned, and fast foods

- Processed vegetable oils (i.e. canola, vegetable, etc.)

- Frozen processed foods

- Pasteurized milk, yogurt and conventional cheese

- Microwaved food

- Canned food

The Natural Diet (real food)

- Fresh, organic and local fruits and vegetables

- Bone broths

- Grass-fed butter and natural animal fats

- Free-range eggs and animals

- Grass-fed cheese

- Sustainably wild-caught fish

- Organic herbs and spices

- Pure or filtered water (I recommend using a Berkey water filter system)

- Healthy oils, like organic extra virgin olive oil and organic coconut oil

- Raw nuts and seeds (i.e. cashews and hemp seeds)

- Fermented veggies

- Unrefined sugar (raw chocolate, raw honey, and pure maple syrup)

- Traditional cooking (roasting and baking in the oven or cooking on a stovetop)

- Soaked beans and grains (not from a can)

- Unrefined salt (ie: Pink himalayan or sea salt)

Tools for Eating Real Food

The more you practice these tools, the easier it gets. Try not to let this list overwhelm you, and instead let yourself be inspired by the opportunities to feel good! Choose one or two of these tools to begin implementing, and when they feel like second-nature to you, add in another one!

The 80/20 Rule

I personally live by the concept of the 80/20 rule — 80 percent of the time you're eating healthy and nourishing foods and 20 percent of the time you are free (without guilt) to indulge in whatever your taste buds desire that day. Try to avoid creating a label for yourself if you can — you'll be more free to explore when dining with friends and traveling to other countries. Indulging and trying new things is part of life! Try testing new recipes. Purchase new veggies, fruits or cuts of meat you haven't tried before. Allow it to be fun and let yourself be pleasantly surprised at how wonderful these new culinary experiences can truly be. Food is meant to be enjoyed just as much as it is meant to be our medicine!

This rule also applies to the natural diet and the modern diet — sometimes I will use a can of organic black beans and not always soak my own. Other times I will make a processed frozen pizza! The key here is that the majority of your food is considered "real." This is not about eating perfectly. It's not about what you eat sometimes, it's about what you eat most of the time.

Primarily Eat Foods That Don't Have a Label

What if you aimed for 80 percent of what you eat to be whole foods and 20 percent to have a label? Instead of buying pre-made guacamole (which has added fillers and other ingredients you don't want to consume), simply buy a fresh avocado. Mash it with a fork, add salt and pepper, a squeeze of lime, and you have your own, highly nutritious, guac. When you are eating out of a packaged food box, know what the ingredients are. Make sure you can pronounce all the ingredients, and if possible, choose foods that have less than five ingredients total. You want to be like a detective and think critically about the foods that you are eating and putting into your body.

Eat More Veggies

You've likely heard before that if you simply focus on adding more vegetables into your diet, you will improve your overall health and well-being. It really can be this simple: instead of telling yourself you have to restrict or not eat certain foods, focus on what you are *adding* into your diet. How can you add an extra veggie into the meal you are cooking for yourself or ordering? And big tip — veggies with breakfast is a great way to start the day! I like to add a handful of cooked spinach onto my plate with eggs and avocados for breakfast.

Cook at Home

You will change your life if you commit to cooking at home, and you don't have to be a "great cook" to be great at cooking nourishing meals for yourself! Later in this chapter, I will share how to be a pro in the kitchen. For now, know that if you don't typically cook, you can start by taking your time and keeping it simple. The more you cook for yourself, the more comfortable you will feel in the kitchen preparing simple, healthy, and quick meals.

Eat Leftovers for Breakfast and Lunch

I like to keep things simple, and an easy way to do that is to make extra healthy foods when you cook so that you have enough leftovers for the next day. Most foods can be added to an omelet for breakfast or into a salad for lunch.

Another easy trick is to store your leftovers in a mason jar as soon as you finish cooking dinner and plan on tossing it over a bed of greens the next day for lunch or easily reheat it on the stove.

Try New and Easy Recipes

Don't be afraid to find something that you can make easily,

and create several different versions of it for yourself.

Get Rid of Your Microwave

Remember the statement earlier about not eating what your great-grandmother wouldn't recognize? I would like to elaborate on that and recommend you primarily cook food the way your great-grandmother cooked food as well. And I guarantee your great-grandma did not cook with a microwave. We must get back to traditional cooking in order to improve our nutrition!

Not only does food heated in the microwave simply not taste good (in my opinion), but there is evidence that they might destroy nutrients in the food. Technically, cooking any food changes the nutrients in some way, but the faster the cooking method, the more nutrients are destroyed. This means that cooking low and slow seems to be the best way to preserve the most nutrients.[14]

What can you use to reheat your food instead? A conventional oven, a toaster oven, a pan on the stovetop, crockpot, or a convection oven!

Stay Hydrated

Up to 60 percent of the human adult body is water. It's so important that we stay hydrated by drinking plenty of water throughout the day. It's easy to mistake being hungry when we are actually just thirsty! Be conscious of your water quality and consider filtering your water. Drink a large glass of room-temperature, filtered water first thing in the morning before any caffeine or food.

Carry a large glass or stainless steel water bottle with you at all times so you are encouraged to stay hydrated. Everytime you refill your water say a beautiful affirmation such as, *"I feel amazing when I am nourished and hydrated."*

Go Organic

Don't panic, it's organic! Whenever possible, choose organic food over conventional food. To be considered organic, produce must be grown without the use of synthetic fertilizers, synthetic pesticides or genetically modified organisms (GMO). Organic meat must be fed 100 percent organic feed and must have access to the outdoors all year long.

Many people believe that organic foods have a higher nutrient content than conventional. Research has confirmed that organic foods have higher antioxidants than conventional foods (between 19 percent and 69 percent more — which is like eating an additional serving or two of vegetables per day.) Another reason to go organic is to reduce the amount of pesticides that are typically consumed in conventional food. A pesticide is a substance that is used to kill, repel or control certain forms of plant or animal life. Pesticide residue is five times higher in conventional produce according to a 2012 analysis.[15]

The good news is that purchasing organic food doesn't have to be all or nothing. The two lists below will help you to determine when to buy organic and which foods you can pass. The Environmental Working Group (EWG), a company working on pesticide policy since 1993, creates annual updated lists of produce with the most and least amount of pesticides on them. They are called The Dirty Dozen and The Clean Fifteen. I take these lists very seriously and will not purchase any of the items from the dirty dozen if they're not organic!

The Dirty Dozen 2022 List[16]

1. Strawberries

2. Spinach

3. Kale, collard and mustard greens

4. Nectarines

5. Apples

6. Grapes

7. Bell and hot peppers

8. Cherries

9. Peaches

10. Pears

11. Celery

12. Tomatoes

The Clean Fifteen 2022 List[17]

1. Avocados

2. Sweet Corn

3. Pineapples

4. Onions

5. Papayas

6. Sweet peas (frozen)

7. Asparagus

8. Honeydew melon

9. Kiwi

10. Cabbage

11. Mushrooms

12. Cantaloupe

13. Mangoes

14. Watermelon

15. Sweet potatoes

Vegetables Should Take Center Stage

Think of meat and animal products as condiments to the meal — not the center stage. Choose which vegetable you want to shine in whatever you are cooking, and let the meat be the "side dish." Try to aim for a big serving of veggies with each meal, whether cooking at home or dining out.

Avoid Anything That Says Low Fat, No Fat, or Sugar Free

Why, you ask? Because if they are removing the natural fats and sugar from the food, that means they are adding something else to replace it. If you are going to eat organic yogurt, get the full-fat organic yogurt. If you are going to eat some organic ice cream, get the full-fat ice cream, and skip the sugar-free, chemical-laden option.

Swap Your Artificial and Fake Sweeteners for Natural Sugars and Sweeteners

Many people are worried about their caffeine consumption, but I believe that caffeine itself is (usually) not the problem. The problem is what you are drinking *with* the caffeine! Are you adding five packets of artificial sweeteners to each cup of coffee you drink? Or maybe three pumps of sugar-free vanilla syrup into your latte? While I encourage you to reduce your refined sugar intake overall, I urge you to stop consuming artificial sugars today.

Artificial sugars like aspartame, sucralose, ace-K, and saccharin have been debated for years on how damaging their effects really are. Things like sugar-free syrup or diet sodas, for example, contain artificial sugars. If you want to sweeten your food or drinks, consider using a healthy sugar substitute!

- Organic raw honey (local to you is best)

- Stevia

- Dates

- Coconut sugar

- Maple syrup

- Brown rice syrup

- Real fruit jam

Include Lots of Good Fats in Your Diet

Nature doesn't make bad fats, factories do. Our brains are composed of 60 percent fat. This means that our brains need fat to work correctly, and to maintain a healthy brain. Many people are eating plenty of fats, but the fats that they are eating are very unhealthy and cause inflammation. Be aware of the fats that you are consuming and start switching to healthier options to get the brain-boosting power they provide.

Bad Fats

Canola oil	Grapeseed oil
Soybean oil	Margarine
Sunflower oil	Cottonseed oil
Corn oil	Peanut oil
Safflower oil	

Good Fats

Grass-fed butter	Avocado oil
Ghee	Olive oil
Coconut milk	Fish oil
Coconut oil	Eggs

Cook your morning eggs (yes, please eat the yolks) in a spoonful of coconut oil. Top your oats with a pat of grass-fed butter. Toss your root veggies in some organic extra virgin olive oil before roasting them in the oven. Add half of an avocado to anything and instantly increase its nutritional value!

Add Fermented Food to Your Meals

I will be explaining more about why this is so important later on in this section. (Spoiler alert: Eating fermented foods improves your gut health, which improves your mental health!) This could look like adding a spoonful of sauerkraut with eggs and avocados, opting for the fermented coconut yogurt with fruit and nut butter, or a spoonful of kimchi with your chicken, veggies, and rice.

Quality Ingredients > Quantity

I cannot highlight enough just how important the quality of your ingredients are! If you take nothing else from this key other than purchasing higher-quality food items than you usually do, you *will* improve your health and well-being significantly! Nutrition and taste often go hand in hand, foods with more nutrients taste better.

Example 1: It's not the meat that is bad for you; it's the quality of the meat that is bad for you. When you are eating poor-quality meat — meaning it was conventionally grown, pumped with hormones, and fed corn or grain to grow quicker or bigger than naturally found in nature — then you are exposing yourself to consuming those harmful additives as well!

Example 2: An organic bag of spinach is much healthier for you than a non-organic bag of spinach because of its nutrient content, and its lack of pesticides and (potentially) harmful bacteria.

Good: A bag of spinach

Great: An organic bag of spinach

Best: A locally grown bag of organic spinach

Go for quality. This means organic, grass-fed, wild-caught, in-season foods. When you choose better quality foods, you will use less when you are cooking and your dishes will turn out better too. More on that later!

Shop the Outer Edges of Grocery Stores

The outer edges of the grocery store are really all that you need to find real foods; the vegetables, fruits, grass-fed cheese, and meats all live on the outer edges. Stay in those areas.

Consider making grocery shopping a fun ritual that supports

taking care of *you*. What energy are you in when you go grocery shopping? One of stress and something else that you "have to do"? If so, you will bring that negative, low-vibe energy into your food. Allow yourself to feel good and use this affirmation before you go into the grocery store:

"I am so excited and grateful to be spending my time selecting nourishing delicious foods that help me feel, look and be my absolute best from the inside out. I deserve the best!"

Spend a few moments before you leave your house to write a list of foods you'd like to get. Make it an event, grab a beautiful coffee or tea, and enjoy yourself as you shop.

Eat It Over a Bed of Greens

When veggies are lacking from your meals or you want to add some extra nutritional value, simply eat whatever you made over a bed of organic greens! I do this all of the time — with organic pasta, shredded chicken, roasted potatoes — I will eat literally anything over a bed of greens when it's in season. It makes me feel awesome and doesn't require any additional prep! Just grab a handful from your weekly pound of organic greens, set it on your plate, and top it with what you made for dinner.

Reclaim the Lost Art Of Cooking

As they say in West Africa, "If you sit at my table and eat with me, you'll know who I am." What does your kitchen table say about you? Eating well is really important for your physical and mental well-being, and it begins with eating at home and cooking for yourself! For some reason, people see cooking for themselves as a big ordeal that has to take hours. I don't believe this to be true. The secret is to keep it simple. Don't make it complicated. Chop up some veggies, toss them with olive oil and spices, and roast in the oven. Done. Throw real food in the crockpot in the morning, and serve dinner when you're ready. Brown some ground beef in a cast-iron skillet, add some seasonally chopped veggies, whatever spices you want, top with some grass-fed cheese, and serve.

I want to share a story with you about my own journey to cooking. My mom will be the first to tell you that she doesn't know where I learned to cook, but that I can cook. My husband will also tell you that I am a talented cook. I used to run a healthy living blog called Alisha's Appetite, where I created and shared healthy recipes with my readers. So, I have to say, I agree with them that I hold my own in the kitchen, but it definitely hasn't always been this way. I taught myself how to cook! I did this by being willing to try new things in the kitchen, watching the Food Network in college, and by wanting to cook the veggies I was buying at the farmer's market. Also, years and years of practice. Once you commit to cooking for yourself and your family, you just get better at it. It gets easier. Plus, you will find more enjoyment in it.

Some of my favorite meals are the easiest meals to prepare. I've even had people ask me for my recipes, and when I list out less than five ingredients, they don't believe me! This is because when you use quality ingredients, you need less ingredients to make a delicious meal! The smaller the ingredient list, the easier it is for you. It's easier to digest, it's easier to cook, and it's easier (and cost effective!) for you to purchase high-quality food.

When I was in graduate school I found ways to keep a tight budget and still purchase healthy options. I would buy pounds of dried beans and cook with meat once or twice a week. When something is important to you and you truly believe in the benefits, you will do whatever it takes to make it happen. And I'm here to tell you there's always a way.

Cook to Change Your Life: How to Be a Pro in the Kitchen

What do you think is the single most important action you can take to experience a healthier diet? Research shows that the answer is simple — a human being, not a machine, should be cooking your food! If you change nothing about your diet, except make a rule that you will eat what you cook, you will see huge, lasting changes in this area of your well-being. Here are some of my best tips for becoming a pro at cooking real food for yourself and your family in the kitchen.

Keep It Clean and Well Stocked

Keep a clean kitchen so that you will want to cook when it's time. Want to eat more greens, local veggies, and healthy fats instead of the ice cream, pre-made meals, and canned soup? Then remove those things from your kitchen entirely. Only keep in it what you are happy feeding your body. Store your nuts, dried beans, and oats in clear mason jars so you can easily see what you have available. (For my must-have kitchen appliances, head to www.alishaleytem.com).

Meal Plan on Sundays

One thing I like to do is stand in my kitchen on Sundays and look through what I have in the cupboards, freezer, and fridge. I keep a large magnetic white board on my fridge, and based on what we have, I list out some meal ideas for the upcoming week. From there, I will place an online order for the rest of my groceries. Look in your fridge, your freezer, and your pantry to see what you already have to base your meals around. Your family will love seeing what's on the menu and it's one less thing for you to think about each day!

Season Your Food

Please stop making bland food! (You will thank me later.) The trick is to season your food multiple times while you are cooking (meaning, a big pinch of pink himalayan sea salt and fresh organic ground pepper multiple times). Do not underestimate the power of high quality salt and pepper. Be sure to include lots of fresh onion, garlic, ginger and organic spices in your cooking, too. Spices are incredibly healthy for you; they can be full of antioxidants, anti-inflammatory, able to balance blood sugar levels, lower cholesterol levels, and so much more. Some of my favorite spices are: chili powder, cinnamon, cumin, turmeric, cayenne, peppercorns, ginger, oregano, black pepper, rosemary, coriander seeds, cloves — the list is endless.

Clean Your Produce

A fun and healthy way to clean your produce is to do a "Veggie Soak." Gather the produce you are eating for the day into a bowl while you make your morning coffee. Fill the bowl with cold water, add a splash of vinegar and 2–3 drops of lemon essential oil (just make sure your oil is a pure essential oil and not a fragrance oil). Citrus oils are natural cleansers and perfect for removing dirt, residue, and chemicals from the skin of your produce! Let sit for five minutes, rinse, and enjoy. This is one of my favorite kitchen rituals and I do this before cooking with my veggies, especially with the veggies I get from my Community Supported Agriculture (CSA) — they are covered in dirt from the earth and I absolutely love seeing it! If you haven't heard of CSA before, I will share more on what that is in the coming pages.

Cook 20-Minute Meals

Get really good at cooking quick meals. Here are some ideas.

Brown some grass-fed ground beef in a cast-iron skillet with some chopped onion, garlic, and peppers. Add a few dashes of cumin, chili powder, oregano, salt, and pepper (eyeball it). Serve the mixture over a bed of greens, a fresh tomato if in season, and top with half of an avocado and a squeeze of lime.

In the morning, add some large sweet potatoes to a crockpot and cook on low for a few hours (depending on how large your potatoes are). When you are ready to eat, stuff the sweet potatoes with shredded chicken, spinach, carrots, and top with a peanut sauce!

Master Making Bone Broth

Bone broth is a highly nutritious food that you will want to add to your diet. The animal bones used to make the broth contain minerals we need to strengthen our bones. It's easy for our bodies to absorb and digest, it strengthens our immune system, and it gives us an amazing source of collagen.

An easy way to get your bone broth each week is to cook a whole, organic, free-range chicken in an Instant Pot. When the chicken is cooked, remove the meat from the bones, place the carcass back into the Instant Pot or pressure cooker, and add some filtered water to cover the bones with a dash of apple cider vinegar (the ACV helps to draw the nutrients out from the bones). I also keep most of my veggie scraps in a freezer bag throughout the week. I will add whatever is in that bag to the pot, along with lots of sea salt and whole garlic cloves. Cook on high pressure for two hours and you have some bone broth! I store mine in a very large mason jar and keep it in the fridge, and use it to make a nutritious soup the following days.

Make It a Meditation

While we will discuss meditation more deeply in another chapter, you can practice meditation (by focusing your mind on what you're doing) while you're cooking. I look forward to cooking at the end of the day and let it be a process of shifting out of work mode and into nourishment mode. I turn on music, start a fire, and let myself get lost in the cooking process of chopping, searing, and mixing. The chopping of veggies with some relaxing music playing in the background, some candles lit or essential oils diffusing, and sometimes even a glass of wine can be a true mindful moment. Let it be fun and remind yourself that you are cooking to nourish your whole self.

Eating as Nature Intended

Think back to the last grocery shopping haul you purchased. Have you ever thought about where each item of food came from? Who grew it, where it came from, when it grew, and how it came to be in your kitchen? I urge you to start thinking more about the quality of your food sources. (Some research is suggesting that the quality is even more important than the quantity of food you eat!)

When you acknowledge where your food comes from, suddenly the food becomes bigger than food. You start to view it differently by having a newfound sense of gratitude for it. And when you start to eat foods that are in season (meaning they grow naturally in a particular season), you become more deeply connected to the earth. You'll find that you respect the food more!

The earth is the ultimate healer, nurturer, and supporter. You might not have grown up thinking or experiencing this, and that's okay. What we can all agree on is that nature knows what's up! She knows what vitamins and nutrients will best support your body. She knows that your body craves an abundance of greens and detoxifying herbs after a long winter. She understands that you need more hydration in the summer due to the heat and provides you with high-water-content veggies that don't require any cooking, like cucumbers and watermelons. She understands that giving you butternut and spaghetti squashes, which require a very warm oven for a longer period of time is just what you need as the weather gets cool every autumn. When you are in tune with what nature has to offer you , when you eat what is in season, you are more in tune with the rhythms of the earth.

The easiest way to eat seasonally is to 1) grow it yourself, 2) shop at a farmers' market each week, or 3) find a local CSA farm to partner with. Remember that CSA stands for *Community Support Agriculture*. Here's how it works: a farmer or homesteader receives a small amount of money from many different "members" who enroll with them to purchase a particular amount of shares each season. With this money, they plant, grow, and harvest the food. The members share the great return of food (or if it's a bad weather year, the small return) together. You can choose to get a family-size share or a half of a share depending on your own family's needs. You can find a local farmer who participates in the CSA program at https://www.localharvest.org/csa/.

Have you ever said something like, "I love my grandmother's cinnamon rolls — I can feel the love she puts into baking them!'"? This is because it actually *is* infused with love! Food has a vibration and an energy to it. Yes, vibration and energy are very real things! Farmers who grow your food have a profound appreciation for the land and the abundance of nourishment it produces for us. You will notice a difference in the produce you buy from a farmer who grows love in with the food vs. purchasing grocery store produce that was mass-produced without this intention of love and appreciation.

Part of eating seasonally is eating new-to-you fruits and vegetables; it's part of the gig. Eating in season means eating what is available! When there is an abundance of zucchini in the summer, you should eat zucchini. When there is more than enough butternut squash in the fall and winter, you should eat the butternut squash. Trust that Mother Nature knows what you need to be nourished. Be open to experimenting and learning new ways to cook new things. Find gratitude for what is available and notice its utmost abundance for you!

Suggestions for Eating Seasonally

- Familiarize yourself with foods that are available in each season.

- Sign up for a CSA share.

- Shop at your local farmer's market.

- If eating out, ask about what seasonal dishes are available.

- Choose which vegetable you are going to base your

home-cooked meal around.

- Refrain from regularly purchasing fruits and veggies that are not in season.

- Learn how to cook simple and seasonal meals.

Below, you can find a list of foods that are abundant in season, and a simple meal idea for each one! What else can you add to the list?

Seasonal Produce and Simple Meal Ideas

SPRING

What's in Season: Arugula, asparagus, green onions, leeks, lettuce, maple syrup, mint, mushrooms, new potatoes, peas, radishes, rhubarb, spinach, strawberries, swiss chard

Breakfast: *Eggs and Greens*

For a single serving, cook 2 eggs in coconut oil. Set them on a plate and then add a couple of big handfuls of spinach to the hot pan and stir until just wilted. Serve the eggs with ½ an avocado, the cooked spinach, a spoonful of homemade sauerkraut and freshly sliced strawberries.

Lunch: *Greens and Sausage Frittata*

Preheat the oven to 350 degrees Fahrenheit. In a hot cast-iron skillet, brown a pound of ground organic sausage. Meanwhile, beat a dozen eggs in a bowl with lots of salt and pepper. Once the meat is cooked through, add a bunch of chopped swiss chard and a big handful of fresh herbs (any that are in season — lemon balm, for example), and toss until wilted. Then add the eggs with salt and pepper to taste. Put the skillet filled with the mixture into the oven and bake for 20–25 minutes, or until the eggs are set. You can top with some grass-fed cheese (optional) and serve with sauerkraut.

Dinner: *Mushroom Pasta with Greens*

Cook a pound of chopped mushrooms with diced onion in a hot cast-iron skillet with a couple tablespoons of melted grass-fed butter. Once cooked, add lots of fresh garlic and a handful of any fresh herbs you have on hand. Meanwhile, cook half a pound of pasta in a pot of salted water. When cooked, use a slotted spoon to remove the pasta directly from the pot and add it to the cast iron with the veggies. Some of the starchy water from the pasta will be added to the skillet with this method, which will act as the sauce! Mix it all together and add lots of freshly shredded cheese (it will melt as you stir). Serve on top of a bed of seasonal greens.

SUMMER

What's in Season: Artichoke, basil, bell peppers, blackberries, blueberries, broccoli, cherries, cilantro, corn, cucumbers, dill, eggplant, fennel, green beans, kale, kohlrabi, lettuce, melon, okra, peaches, plums, potato, red onion, tomatoes, summer squash, zucchini

Breakfast: *Chia Seed Pudding*

Mix together ½ cup of full-fat coconut milk and 2 tablespoons of chia seeds until very well combined. Add a dash of salt and a drizzle of honey or maple syrup. Let the mixture sit in the fridge overnight. In the morning, add a ¼ cup of plain organic kefir or nut milk and add your favorite toppings! I love to add toasted organic coconut flakes, hemp seeds, pumpkin seeds, and blueberries. This breakfast is best served with iced coffee and eaten outside in the grass in the morning summer sun.

Lunch: *Tuna Salad with Sliced Cucumber*

Add to a bowl 1 can of sustainable wild-caught tuna, 1 tablespoon of tahini paste, a squeeze of half a lemon, 1 tablespoon of extra virgin olive oil, a clove of minced garlic, a handful of freshly chopped basil, and sea salt and pepper. Serve the tuna mix with some sliced cucumbers, freshly sliced tomatoes, and a handful of olives. Drizzle organic olive oil and squeeze the other half of the lemon over the top of the entire meal. Use the cucumbers as "chips" to eat the tuna.

Dinner: *Greek Chicken Salad*

Marinate 1 pound of organic chicken breasts or thighs with 2 tablespoons of organic extra virgin olive oil, 2 large cloves of minced garlic, the juice of one lemon, a teaspoon of dried oregano (or tablespoon of fresh oregano), and salt and pepper for at least 30 minutes and up to 24 hours. Grill the chicken breasts until cooked thoroughly. Slice the chicken breasts and top over a bed of greens with chopped tomatoes, fennel, cucumbers, red onions, olives, feta cheese, and more fresh oregano. Squeeze lots of fresh lemon over the top and add a few drizzles of organic olive oil. Serve with hummus and pita bread. Eat outside as the sun sets.

FALL

What's in Season: Apples, broccoli, brussels sprouts, cauliflower, celery, collards, cranberries, grapes, kale, pear, parsnips, persimmons, pumpkin, spaghetti squash, swiss chard, sweet potatoes, winter squash

Breakfast: *Brussels Sprout Hash*

Add 1 big tablespoon of coconut oil to a hot cast-iron skillet. Add 1 cup of sliced brussels sprouts, salt and pepper, and cook until they turn bright green. Remove the brussels sprouts and in the same pan, cook 2 eggs over easy. Top the brussels sprouts with the eggs and serve with half of an avocado and lots of hot sauce.

Lunch: *Roasted Root Veggies and Chicken*

Roast a variety of root vegetables (such as sweet potatoes, carrots, and parsnips) on a big sheet pan for 20–25 minutes at 425 degrees Fahrenheit with olive oil and spices of choice. Chop the veggies to be the same size. Cook a whole chicken in an instant pot on high pressure for 28 minutes. Serve pieces of chicken with the root veggies and a drizzle of tahini and lemon juice on top.

Dinner: *Beef Bolognese Stuffed Spaghetti Squash*

Brown 1 pound of grass-fed beef in a hot cast-iron skillet with a chopped onion. Add 1 jar of marinara sauce (or make your own!). Meanwhile, cut a spaghetti squash in half and add to an instant pot with 1 cup of water. Cook on high pressure for 8 minutes. Scoop the squash out of the skin, top with the beef bolognese sauce, and top with lots of shredded organic grass-fed cheese.

WINTER

What's in Season: Apples, beets, cabbage, carrots, citrus, onions, parsnips, potatoes, pomegranates, rutabagas, sweet potatoes, turnips

Breakfast: *Soaked Oats*

My go-to breakfast in the winter is a big warm bowl of oats cooked in coconut milk! To help with digestion, soak 1 cup of rolled oats in filtered water overnight. In the morning, drain the water and add the oats to a small oat cooker (a small device that can cook grains such as rice or oats). Add ½ cup of coconut milk and ½ cup of filtered water, a pinch of salt, a drizzle of maple syrup, ¼ cup of hemp seeds, and any fruit you have on hand (I usually use frozen fruit in the winter). Cook for 15–20 minutes. Serve with nut butter and chia seeds on top.

Lunch: *Taco Soup*

This is a really fast and easy soup that doesn't take very long to make. I like to make it for lunch and leave it on the stove to reheat and eat again for dinner! Dice up one onion and saute it in a large pot. Add 1 pound of ground organic chicken and 3–5 cloves of fresh garlic. Add a can of organic black beans, a can of organic diced tomatoes, frozen corn and lots of chili powder and cumin. Simmer it all in a bone broth until cooked and serve with a squeeze of lime, avocado, shredded cheese, cilantro, red onion, and pickled jalapenos.

Dinner: *Chicken and Fries*

Chop large sweet potatoes to look like french fries. Mix with melted coconut oil and salt and pepper. While they bake in the oven at 425 degrees Fahrenheit, sear a pound of organic chicken thighs in a hot cast-iron skillet with a couple table-spoons of butter and salt and pepper until crispy. Serve with a spoonful of sauerkraut (sauerkraut is fermented cabbage and a great source of probiotics with a distinct sour taste).

The Link Between a Healthy Gut and a Healthy Mind

When we eat a lot of veggies, we have more healthy bacteria in our gut. The healthier your diet is, the healthier your gut is. Research has recently confirmed what holistic medicine has known for thousands of years — that the gut is considered our "second brain." Did you know that you can assess your gut health by looking at your poop? That's right! I know this can get a little awkward talking about your bowels, but we have to go there.

Your poop is giving you a glimpse into what's working and not working with both your diet and your ability to "digest" your emotions. A recent study shows that people who are anxious and depressed have higher rates of constipation.[18] This means that stress and emotions greatly affect your large intestine. When we hold on to things that we can't let go of or internalize our struggles (meaning, we don't express our emotions), our bodies hold onto stress in our organs and we can become majorly constipated or have other digestive issues.

The Greek philosopher Hippocrates and ancient Ayurvedic Medicine both stated that all disease begins in the gut. We know today that 70 to 80 percent of our immune system is in our gut, so it's very important to poop daily. If you don't, those toxins stay in your body and can create inflammation. This means that when you are constipated, your body is essentially absorbing your poop and keeping all of those toxins inside of your body. I will share my holistic remedies for constipation shortly, but first it's important to know that we can assess our gut health by looking in the toilet.

The Perfect Poop

The Bristol Stool Chart was developed as a reference tool to demonstrate what healthy stools look like. As you can see on the following chart, types 1 and 2 from the scale indicate constipation. Types 3 and 4 are the ideal stools. And types 5 through 7 are leaning toward diarrhea.

The Bristol Stool Chart[19] offers a picture of where you are in regards to your lifestyle and nutrition choices, but it is not the ultimate proof of your digestive health. Use it as a reference point to where you are more often than not, and then use the tools you are learning in this chapter to support you!

Bristol Stool Chart

Type 1		Separate hard lumps, like nuts (hard to pass)
Type 2		Sausage-shaped, but lumpy
Type 3		Like a sausage, but with cracks on its surface
Type 4		Like a sausage or snake, smooth and soft
Type 5		Soft blobs with clear-cut edges (passed easily)
Type 6		Fluffy pieces with ragged edges, a mushy stool
Type 7		Watery, no solid pieces ENTIRELY LIQUID

The Perfect Poop

- Occurs first thing in the morning (before eating breakfast and without the help of coffee). After your morning stool, you should feel light, energetic and like it's all out. This should feel like a relieving sensation. It shouldn't be painful, though some urgency is normal.

- Your poop should be solid but soft (see types 3 – 4 in the bristol chart).

- Easy to wipe and not super smelly.

- Looks like the shape of a banana with the tip at the end.

- Should be the same consistency every morning.

More Probiotics, Please

Trillions of bacteria and other microbes live in your gut to help you digest your food and contribute to your health. Microbes live in the gut (known as the gut microbiome), and your microbiome affects how you respond to food. The path to having a healthy gut microbiome is to have diverse microbes, and you can improve microbe diversity by the foods that you eat — specifically by consuming both a variety of foods and probiotics to influence the bacteria in your gut.[20]

You may have noticed I have talked about consuming fermented foods several times in this chapter so far — this is because fermented foods naturally contain probiotics. The most common fermented foods that contain probiotics are: kefir, sauerkraut, kimchi, sourdough starter, and kombucha. According to the Founder and President of the Weston A. Price Foundation (a foundation dedicated to returning nutrient-dense foods to the American diet through education, research, and activism), Sally Fallon Morell states, "There are more beneficial bacteria in a spoonful of raw sauerkraut than there are in a whole bottle of probiotic pills."[21] Isn't that amazing?

But if you aren't eating enough fermented foods in your diet, you can still supplement with probiotics. Be sure to do your research before you purchase supplements, as there are many different strains of bacteria and you want to be sure you are getting a high-quality strain. If you are unsure, talk to your doctor about what they recommend for you.

If you choose supplements in order to get your probiotics in, the best time to take your probiotic is on an empty stomach, preferably right before bed. This gives the bacteria a chance to work through your large intestine and do the most good. If you do this, you might notice that you are able to have beautiful morning poops!

The Impact of Stress and Your Emotions

Have you ever noticed that when you are feeling constipated or backed up you also tend to feel stuck in a particular area of your life? During stressful times, it's common to hold on to our poop. According to Traditional Chinese Medicine, holding on to past memories or emotions can lead to anxiety and amplify stress. When the large intestine (known as our garbage collector) is out of balance, it's associated with an inability to grieve and let go, which shows up as constipation.

We need to work with our emotions to have better gut health. We must learn to manage and handle the daily stressors of life in a form of healthy expression instead of suppression. Identify what you are holding onto emotionally — is there an event in your life, a person, relationship, job, etc. that you are having a very difficult time letting go of?

Knowing how to calm your nervous system is vital to improving your health and well-being. When we know how to relax, we are taking our nervous system from "fight or flight" into "rest and digest." When we rest the mind and physical body, our organs relax and are able to digest and poop!

Tracking Your Nutrition for a Healthier Gut

Use this tracker for one week to help you be conscious of your gut health by tracking the real foods and fermented foods you eat, your stress levels, and your stool type. You will begin to see patterns and insights that you can then make improvements upon. And don't forget to aim for 80 percent of your meals to be real and seasonal.

Day of Week	Real and Seasonal Foods Consumed	Processed Foods Consumed	Fermented Foods Consumed	*Stool Type (1–7)*	Stress Level 1–10 (1 = Low, 10 = High)
Sunday					
Monday					
Tuesday					
Wednesday					
Thursday					
Friday					
Saturday					

After one week, grab your journal and reflect with the following prompts:

- What patterns are you seeing in your meals? What percentage of the time do you cook? What meal of the day is the most difficult for you to eat healthy? Start with that meal and focus on adding more veggies into it.

- How would you like to consume probiotics? (ie: through fermented foods or supplements?)

- How much water are you consuming each day?

Holistic Remedies to Improve Your Digestion

Positive Self-Talk

Hay House Founder Louise Hay created the perfect affirmation for breaking free of digestive issues: *"I digest life and assimilate all new experiences peacefully and joyously."* Everytime you finish a bowel movement, thank yourself for letting go! I realize this might feel silly the first time you do it as a grown adult, but believe me, it helps you tune into your body and its natural processes that keep you functioning at your highest potential! Your mind and body are always connected — including your bowel movements. I like to thank my body everytime I finish going to the bathroom for letting go of what no longer serves me because on an emotional level, pooping is just that...letting go. Have some FUN with it!

A Detox Salt Bath

Epsom salts can help the body and gut relax and soften your stool when your skin absorbs them in a warm bath. Epsom salts are pure magnesium, and can attract more fluid to your bowels. This extra fluid stretches the intestines and helps to move the stool along. Be sure to purchase a bag of pure quality Epsom salts, preferably without anything else added to them (including any fragrances that are often disguised as essential oils).

How to Take a Salt Bath:

1. Run a bath with very warm water (as warm as you can stand).

2. Add 1 cup of Epsom salts into the warm bath. You can also add a couple drops of relaxing essential oils to the salts, such as lavender or frankincense. Stay safe by adding the oils directly to the salts to solubilize for five minutes before adding them to the water.

3. Soak in the bath for 20–30 minutes. Do this before bed and you will likely be constipation-free in the morning!

Warm Lemon Water

Drinking warm water with lemon first thing in the morning on an empty stomach can stimulate your digestive system and get the juices flowing for the day. Squeeze half of a fresh lemon into 8–10 ounces of warm water (not boiling — remove the kettle before it begins to boil!) Drink it entirely before moving onto breakfast or coffee. This will get things going in the gut for the day and give you a boost of Vitamin C!

Supplementation

- **Triphala:** Triphala is a traditional Ayurvedic medicine that is often used to treat constipation. Take two capsules of triphala with warm water at bedtime.

- **Digestive Enzymes:** Take a good-quality digestive enzyme with your meals to support better digestion of the food. I personally like to take digestive enzymes when I am eating processed foods, such as pizza on Friday nights!

- **Magnesium Bath Flakes or Epsom Salts:** Magnesium bath flakes (magnesium chloride) help your muscles to relax, and therefore support digestion. You can take a warm bath with 1 cup of Epsom salts to get magnesium in through your skin. You can find Epsom salts at the grocery store, a health-food store, or online.

- **Probiotics:** As I mentioned earlier, you can choose to take a probiotic supplement in place of eating enough fermented foods.

- **Ginger:** There's plenty of evidence that ginger aids digestion. Drink ginger tea after completing a meal to support stomach discomfort. Simply drinking organic ginger tea (or even tea with minced fresh ginger) throughout the day will help as well.

Eat More Cooked Veggies (Less raw veggies)

Sometimes we can do more harm by eating too many raw foods with high fiber content. More veggies are good and when it comes to your digestive health, *cooked* veggies are great! Give your gut some support by eating more cooked vegetables, and be sure to cook them in a good-quality source of fat such as grass-fed butter.

Yoga for Healthy Digestion

These yoga poses help to lower your cortisol levels and bring your nervous system into "rest and digest" mode to regulate your bowel movements. Consistent, gentle movement that feels good is really all you need. Practice these simple yoga poses to support your digestion after a meal or at any time of day.

Knees to Belly

This is known as the "wind-reliev-ing pose." Lie on your back and hug the knees comfortably to the belly. Stay here for 5–10 full breaths. With your knees at your chest, roll onto your left side and stay lying on your stomach for 5–10 breaths.

Seated Twist

Detoxifying twists in yoga help to stimulate the colon, ushering toxins out and aiding in diges-tion. In a cross-legged seat, take your right hand and place it on your left knee. Place your left hand on the ground behind your left hip. With a straight spine, inhale and gently twist your spine, looking over your left shoulder. Stay for 5–10 full breaths. Repeat on the other side.

Child's Pose

Child's pose compresses the stomach and massages the internal organs, stimulating the digestive system. Come to kneel on the knees and sit back onto the heels. Bringing your knees comfortably wide, fold over the legs and rest your forehead on the floor. Either place your hands back by the feet or stack them under the forehead as a little pillow. Deeply inflate your lower belly against your upper thighs with each breath, and remain here for 5–10 full breaths.

A Summary of How to Unlock The Gold Key of Nutrition

1. Become aware of your food intake and determine if what you are eating is considered real food.

2. Familiarize yourself with what foods are in season and purchase your foods locally (grow it yourself, buy from a farmer's market, or become a CSA member).

3. Focus on adding more vegetables to your meals (the golden amount is five servings of veggies and fruit per day).

4. Embrace the lost art of cooking your own food. If you do nothing else but cook your own food, you will greatly improve your nutrition intake!

5. Be aware of your stool everyday, and be proactive in maintaining a healthy gut.

Affirmations for the Gold Key of Nutrition

- I feel amazing when I stay hydrated and well nourished.

- Planning healthy meals for the week feels so good.

- I choose to eat real food.

- I am capable of cooking fast, healthy, and delicious meals.

- I am worth the time and money I invest in my health.

- I am able to balance my life and find time to cook nourishing healthy food.

- I know how to relax and support my digestion.

- I am so grateful for the people who grew this food, the people who transported this food, and the people who prepared this food.

- I bless this food and my body with love.

Turn Your Nutrition Intake into G.O.L.D.

Grab your journal and use these prompts to reflect on your next steps for unlocking this key:

G: What's **going well** with your nutrition?

O: What **obstacles** are you facing with your nutrition intake?

L: What are you **learning** about your relationship with food from this chapter?

D: What will you **do** to improve your nutrition intake moving forward?

If you want to dive deeper into the concepts of this chapter, here are some recommended books:

- *Go with Your Gut* by Robyn Youkilis

- *Loving Yourself To Great Health* by Louise Hay, Ahlea Khadro, and Heather Dane

- *Simply in Season* by Cathleen Hockman-Wert and Mary Beth Lind

- *Food Rules* by Michael Pollan

- *Happy, Healthy, Sexy* by Katie Silcox

Next we will share how movement not only supports a healthy body but can help you to be happier, more clear-minded, and aware.

"Blessed are the flexible, for they shall not be bent out of shape."
– Unknown

"To enjoy the glow of good health, you must exercise."
– Gene Tunney

"Physical fitness is not only one of the most important
keys to a healthy body; it is the basis of a dynamic and
creative intellectual activity."
– John F. Kennedy

CHAPTER 3

The Third Key: Movement

The gold key of movement is the practice of activating the physical body to promote health across the entire body.

I believe most people don't know how good they can feel in their bodies. Not feeling pain isn't the same as feeling good. Feeling good physically is about feeling strong, limber, and confident in your body. Notice how I say *feeling* and not *looking*, because unlocking this key is not about how you look — it's about how you *feel*. This is the essence of the gold key of movement: when you regularly move your body, you feel good.

I have to admit, I know what it feels like to have massive resistance to moving my body. My relationship with movement hasn't always been positive. I used to loathe "working out" and saw it as a chore. Thinking about going to the gym bored me. I always thought I had better and more fun things to do and resisted formally exercising at all costs.

Now, however, I have a very positive relationship with moving my body. It started with thinking differently about movement and changing my relationship to exercise. Now, I look forward to this time of my day, as I see it as my own self-care time. It's time that I make just for me, to take amazing care of myself. How would you prioritize more movement if you viewed it as an act of self-care?

You're reading this book right now because you're ready to improve your well-being and are willing to do what it takes to create this for yourself. You wouldn't have made it this far in the book if you weren't serious about making the changes necessary to live a happier and healthier life. I want to help you think differently about exercise! Let's start with why you might want to make being active a core part of who you are. And yes, it *is* possible for you no matter what your relationship with exercise has been like so far.

The world is becoming more virtual than ever, and year by year, people are spending the majority of their time sitting in front of a screen. So much time is spent living from our heads that we are neglecting our bodies. Have you ever worked at your computer for so long that you forgot to eat lunch? That's an example of being in your head and not in your body.

All of this excess screen time means that we are sitting more than ever before, and too much sitting is not good for our health and well-being. Recent studies show that one in four Americans spend more than eight hours a day sitting. They are also finding that people who sit for more than seven hours a day are much more likely to develop depression, dementia, and Alzheimer's.[22]

The problem with sitting (or inactivity) is that the decrease in blood circulation makes it harder for happiness hormones like endorphins, dopamine, and serotonin to reach your receptors. Research has found that sitting for long periods of time is harmful — some scientists even say that sitting is the new smoking. The good news is that 60 to 75 minutes of moderately intense physical activity a day counters the effects of too much sitting![23]

Women are more likely than men to be less active. I personally believe this is because women tend to put themselves last to make sure everyone around them is taken care of. We are nurturers at heart and strive to take care of those we love, often at the expense of our own health and well-being. The better you take care of yourself, the better you are able to take care of those around you. You are in charge of how great you take care of yourself — nobody else can do it for you.

Surprising Reasons to Move Every Day

It's easy to focus on why we *don't* want to move our bodies, and what we focus on grows. So, let's focus on all of the reasons you might *want* to move your body.

It Makes You Genuinely Happier

Move your body more and you will become happier! Movement creates blood flow, which stimulates the production of endorphins, chemicals in the brain that are the body's natural painkillers and mood elevators. People underestimate how much happier they become simply from regularly exercising, but it will genuinely make you happier and improve your mental health. Numerous studies have shown that people who exercise regularly experience fewer symptoms of depression and anxiety than those who do not. Now, you can be *that* person who says, "I'm going to release some endorphins," and move your body to do so. And it does *not* have to include going to the gym!

It Boosts Your Confidence

When you are working out, your brain releases a protein called BDNF (Brain-Derived Neurotrophic Factor), which protects the brain from stress and acts as a reset switch. This is why we feel so at ease, clear, and confident after working out.

Moving your body activates your physical core, also known as the energy center that governs your self-esteem and confidence. When you move your body in ways that are out of your comfort zone, you are increasing your levels of self-esteem! I've said it before and I'll say it again: when you feel good, you look good. When you feel good, you show up with more confidence in your life.

It Relieves Stress and Gets You Out of Your Head

When you are experiencing stress, your body goes into what's called the "fight-or-flight response." Exercising helps your body to get out of "fight-or-flight" mode and instead regulates the nervous system. Simply moving mitigates the effects of stress on your body and at the same time improves the function of your bodily systems like the cardiovascular, immune, and digestive systems.

Increases Creativity and Focus

Researchers are confirming that they have found a link between an active lifestyle and creativity! Regularly exercising helps you to think outside of the box and improves innovative thinking. This is another reason why organizations should be encouraging their employees to work out during their workday to help foster greater innovation.

Helps You to Stay Physically Fit and Improves Overall Health

The link between physical exercise and improved health — in both body and mind — is long established and nothing new. However, sometimes it helps to remember the basics: if you want to be healthier, move more!

It Reduces Fatigue and Gives You Energy

The psychological part of exercise has been shown to directly correlate with energy levels — you feel better and have more energy. The best way to burn off stress hormones without having to change your thinking is to move and sweat.

Improves Your Immune System

Having just experienced the COVID-19 pandemic, it's imperative that we all do what we can to strengthen our immune systems! When you are under stress, your immune system is suppressed because stress impacts cortisol and cortisol influences the immune system. A simple fix to help with everyday stresses and keep a strong immune system is to workout. Studies even show that regular exercise slows down the aging process by keeping the immune system young!

Check Your Mindset: Why Don't You Want to Move?

I can tell you all of the benefits and reasons why you should work out (and you likely know a lot of them), but you may still find yourself not doing it. As I have been repeating throughout this book, your mindset and thoughts will dictate the actions you take. Therefore, the more positive thoughts you think about movement, the more you'll find yourself taking the action and moving your body.

I want you to be a detective and start to think about your own relationship with moving your body. What's the first thing that comes to mind when you hear the phrases "move your body" or "workout"? Do you despise the thought of working out? Are you not loving reading this key in the book? Do you feel ashamed or embarrassed thinking about moving your body? If you struggle with regular movement, finish this statement by choosing the ones that you think the most. "Exercise is..."

- A thing I don't have time for!

- Something I have to do to lose weight.

- Hard and sweaty.

- Not much fun.

- For athletes and flexible people.

- Something I'm not good at.

- Something I'm embarrassed or self-conscious about.

- Something I can't stick to.

- For people who can afford personal trainers.

- Something for younger people.

Grab the journal you've been using throughout this book and take a moment to reflect on your relationship to movement with these prompts:

- What is my relationship to exercise? What do I believe it means or doesn't mean?

- What comes up for me when I hear the phrase: "You make time for what is important to you"?

- Why **don't** I want to move my body? What do I gain by staying sedentary or staying at my desk for long hours at a time?

- How do I physically feel in my body?

- How can I bring attention to the parts of my body that don't feel good after I work out? What else might be there?

The above questions are designed to help uncover what

self-limiting beliefs are holding you back. Now that you've identified some thoughts you have about movement, let's dive into how to make over your mind with your relationship to moving your body.

How to Make Over Your Mind about Movement

Think of Movement as Daily Medicine

Knowing all of the benefits that movement offers you, start to look at daily exercise as your essential medicine. Movement is proven to be an effective treatment for many forms of depression and anxiety. Remind yourself that some kind of movement every day is simply the medicine you need to be and feel your best!

You Need Your Health to Be Successful

Entrepreneur Gary Vaynerchuk was once asked, "How important is your health in business?" He replied, "Well, if you're dead, you're out of business." Without being too morbid, sometimes remembering our mortality is exactly what's needed to start living, and living well.

Move to Bring Joy into Your Life

Use moving your body as a tool to bring even more joy into your life! Moving isn't supposed to be a dreadful experience. It's meant to be uplifting, fun, and energizing! What if you moved just for the sake of celebrating your beautiful body? Here are three ways you can use movement to bring more joy into your life:

1. Remember your favorite childhood movement.

Think back to your childhood: What did you do for fun? Did you explore wooded trails with your friends? Did you love playing a particular sport? Maybe you liked swimming, riding your bike, or playing basketball. I grew up going to gymnastics, so as an adult I love practicing yoga, dance, and lifting weights — all of these exercises bring me back to the fun I had as a young gymnast.

2. Do it with your partner or family.

If you're in a committed relationship or marriage, consider working out with your partner! It can truly be really fun to plan active adventures together. Go on a date to the gym, run a 5k together, or go on a hike! You'll have more fun, bond on a new level, and be healthier together in the long run. Plus, the accountability is a great bonus. These days, my husband and I workout together in our home gym while our daughter plays in her playpen next to us. In between sets, we have a dance party with her. We're creating beautiful memories and uplifting our health, all at the same time!

3. Do something that inspires you.

Have you ever felt inspired by someone doing something adventurous like rock climbing, running a race, or nailing a yoga pose? Let your inspiration guide you — be curious about what you are drawn to and go after it!

Find a Movement Style You Love

Remember, there are endless possibilities for how you can

move your body. All that matters is that you move in some way. "I choose forms of exercise that keep my body strong and healthy. My body responds positively to all kinds of movement," as Louise Hay once said. Your body will respond positively to whatever form of movement you decide to practice. The more you love a movement, the more you will stick with it. If you do it because you think you "should," you are less likely to continue. It's helpful in multiple ways to choose a style of movement that excites you. Check a mark next to all of the following exercises that sound like fun:

_____ Biking

_____ Crossfit

_____ Dance class

_____ Gardening

_____ Group boot camp programs (ie: local YMCA)

_____ HIIT (High Intensity Interval Training)

_____ Hiking trails

_____ Joining a gym

_____ Hot power yoga (a faster-paced style of yoga, usually in a heated room)

_____ Joining a team sport (basketball, soccer, hockey)

_____ Kettlebell training

_____ Pilates

_____ Restorative yoga (relaxing and slow yoga, usually with the use of props)

_____ Rock climbing

_____ Running in a race (5k, 10k, half or full marathon)

_____ Running sprints

_____ Stand-up paddle-board (SUP) yoga

_____ Strength training program

____ Snowboarding   ____ Surfing

____ Snow shoeing   ____ Tai Chi

____ Spin class   ____ Water skiing

____ Swimming   ____ Zumba

_____(write in your own favorite form of movement here)

See Movement as No Big Deal and a Natural Part of Who You Are

This is one of my favorite techniques to use. When we make something a big deal, then our mind tends to see it as hard to achieve or impossible. It's "above" you in a sense. The solution is to take it off of a pedestal and make it no big deal. If you started to see regular exercise as no big deal and a natural part of who you are (of course you are the kind of person who regularly exercises), then it will soon become second nature! I've applied this mindset to so many areas of my life and it serves me very well. Try it!

Motivating Yourself When You Don't Want To Move

I find that when we struggle with trying to "motivate" ourselves to move our bodies, then we are trying to do it for all of the wrong reasons. These reasons tend to be external validation or the desire to look a certain way. This can absolutely motivate some people for a certain period of time, but what's lasting and fulfilling is to move because it feels good. Move because it's benefiting your well-being. Move because you deserve to feel good, have mental clarity, and live a healthy and balanced life. All of the other external reasons (toning up, gaining muscle, losing weight) simply become the cherry on top, not the primary reason or motivation.

A 3-Step Method to Check In with Your Body

You can practice this method when you are unsure of what would be the most beneficial practice for you to do next. You might get the message from your body that it wants to be challenged. You might hear that it wants rest and restorative, gentle movement. The point of this practice is to get really good at identifying and then honoring your own true needs!

Step 1: Sit down where you will be undisturbed for a few minutes. Close your eyes, place one hand over your heart and another on your stomach, and take several deep, cleansing breaths until you feel relaxed.

Step 2: Once you are relaxed and still, scan your body to notice any areas of tension or discomfort. If you are new to the practice of scanning your body, please refer to the gold key of mindfulness to learn more. The short version of this practice is to bring your awareness to each general part of your body and notice the sensations that arise. For example, tune into your upper back and shoulders. How do they feel? Tight? Heavy? Simply notice and be aware.

Step 3: Now that you are in tune with yourself, ask your heart space, "What do you need right now? What style of movement would support you?" The answer may not come right away. That's okay. The answer may be a feeling or sensation. The more you practice this method, the better skilled you will become at knowing when the answer has arrived. The most important part is to honor whatever comes up.

Focus on How It Will Make You Feel

Instead of viewing movement as:

- Punishment

- Something you *should* do

- Something you *need* to do to

....what if you just focused on how moving your body makes you feel?

What if movement was something you did for yourself to feel better physically, mentally, and emotionally?

What if the main goal was to simply...feel good? What if you moved to celebrate what your body can do? What if you released all attachment to moving your body to look a certain way and instead did it to *feel* a certain way?

Sometimes you might be motivated to move your body in order to achieve a certain physical goal you've set. Seeing physical results in your body can be a powerful motivator. This can be great for short-term motivation, but we are interested in *lasting* motivation. I believe you will find this when you focus on how moving makes you feel. When you feel good, you perform better in every area of your life.

If you are struggling to motivate yourself, ask yourself: *How do I want to feel?*

While any form of movement will give you an energy boost, lifting weights typically makes you feel strong. Practicing yoga helps you to feel flexible and open. Walking or running helps you to access that "runner's high." Snowboarding gives you a rush and makes you feel adventurous. Think about how you want to feel and what movement you'd like to engage in to feel that way.

For example: I want to feel strong and confident in my body again after pregnancy and giving birth. In order to feel strong, I will focus on weight lifting to move my body. (This may or may not have been a real-life situation for me!)

Another example: I want to feel relaxed and flexible in my body to manage my stressful workload. To feel relaxed and flexible, I will engage in practicing yoga to move my body.

Your turn: I want to feel _____. To feel this way in my body, I will engage in _____ to move my body.

Mix Up Your Exercise Routine with the Seasons

Our energy changes with the seasons, so it's beneficial to change up your movement with the season. When it's cold in the dead of winter, long, slow movements like yoga are best. When the first sign of life springs up, our bodies crave more energizing and faster movements — such as running a race or taking some group boot camp classes. Summer invites us to play outside: surf in the ocean, run on the trails, or go kayaking. And when the leaves begin to change, we crave new weight-lifting programs or to go for long hikes.

Know the season that you are in. Your body and movement regiment will change like the seasons, depending on what's happening in your life. Are you in the season that's asking you to push out of your comfort zone, expand your body to new heights, and try new, challenging things? Or are you in the season that's asking you to rest, take it easy, and learn how to replenish yourself and your energy? This is why it's important that you stay open to your interests and routines changing over time, because you are changing!

You might have been in a season of loving HIIT workouts, but now can't get into them or stay consistent; this is your body's natural way of telling you she's needing to slow down and wants more nourishing walks and restorative yoga. Have you been on a yoga kick but now it feels dull and uninspiring? This may be your body asking for more intensity and to change it up with something more challenging. (This may still be yoga, but maybe it's a more intense yoga that pushes you out of your comfort zone, or maybe it's taking a break from yoga and going to the weight rack.) Know when you need to challenge yourself with your movements! Knowing what season you are in requires radical honesty and self-awareness. Take a moment to revisit the "3-Step Method to Check in with Your Body" journal prompt with the seasons in mind to gain more insight into where you are now.

Energize Yourself with Aromatherapy

Naturally energize yourself before a workout with a peppermint orange essential oil "bomb." Peppermint oil provides natural energy, and orange oil uplifts your mood. Therefore this is an energy and mood uplifter. Place 1–2 drops of peppermint essential oil and 1–2 drops of orange essential oil onto your palms. Rub the palms together, and then cup your nose, taking in five deep breaths of the energizing aroma. Continue on to your workout with this beautiful boost!

The Gold Movement Trio: Yoga + Weight lifting + Walking

I have discovered a magical trio of movements that offers the perfect blend of variety and health benefits that I refer to as the "Gold Movement Trio." You can add this combination into your routine if you feel called to do so, or use them as a guide to create your own magic trio. Just include some kind of cardio, strength training, and stretching.

Gold Movement Trio #1: Walking

If I had to choose just one form of movement I could do for the rest of my life, I would choose walking. It creates movement across the entire body, and you can do it outside in nature to stack even more health and well-being benefits. (More on the power of nature in the next chapter!)

I take my (almost) daily walks very seriously. Whenever I move to a new area, my neighbors always know me as "the girl who is out walking." When I am on my "A" game, I walk for an hour a day. I've listened to countless books and podcasts while walking outside. I treat my walks as a way to move my body, get into nature, and grow my mind all in one. When I was eight months pregnant, I was still consistently walking one hour a day!

As my life changes, how I'm able to get my walks in changes as well. At one point in my life, I would walk solo or with my husband. When I became a dog owner, I would take my dog on my walks. And then, when I became a mother, I would carry my baby (in a front stomach carrier) and take my dog on my walks. The point is: where there's a will, there's a way. What's important to you will always get done.

A recent study from Stanford University showed that creativity is increased by nearly 60 percent while walking,[24] and another study found that the reason creativity can come through during walks is because the brain's attention span frees up. Have you ever heard someone say, *"I had the best idea on my walk"*? Some of my best solutions and ideas come to me while I am walking! This is why walking is good for business and creative solutions. If I'm stuck on an idea (or in the downward spiral of negative self-talk), I will head outside for an hour of walking.

For some reason, walking is seen as "not counting" for moving your body because it's not running or some other high-intensity movement. I say (and research agrees) that this simply isn't true. If all you do to start moving more is walk for thirty minutes a day, you will see some seriously amazing results! If you need to make a decision or feel creatively stuck, head outside for a walk in the park. Be ready for the solution to come to you.

Plus, you never have to get bored of walking because of all the ways you can mix it up! Walk in a new neighborhood, explore a new trail, or visit a local track at a school. Listen to a variety of things while walking — audiobooks, podcasts, affirmations, or your favorite music. You can walk solo or make it a group activity and walk with others. You can walk while you work (take phone calls, for example), or you can walk after you finish your workday to help you unwind and prepare for your evening.

Try it now: Where can you add walking as part of your day? Can you walk with your kids after dinner instead of watching a TV show? Can you take some work calls while you walk? Can you walk for your commute? Try going for a walk first thing in the morning and watch how your day unfolds. Author Henry Thoreau put it best when he said, "An early morning walk is a blessing for the whole day."[25] I couldn't agree more.

Gold Movement Trio #2: Yoga

It is very common for many to mistakenly think that you have to be flexible to practice yoga. As a certified yoga teacher with hundreds of hours teaching yoga under my belt, I always tell my students that yoga is what helps you to become more limber and flexible, and that you don't have to be either of those things when you begin.

To me, yoga is not about becoming more flexible. Yoga is to help me calm my nervous system and connect to my true self! It's the *ultimate* mind-body movement, and I always feel a million times better walking away from my mat than when I started. Yoga changed my life, and I am forever grateful for all that it has taught, and continues to teach, me about myself.

There are so many benefits to yoga as a legitimate exercise for both the body *and* the mind. Whether you are a longtime yogi or a total newbie, yoga is an awesome way to get sweaty and centered at the same time. There are so many benefits to practicing yoga, but here are a few of the most impressive ones:

Releases Tight Muscles

Stress and anxiety can leave our bodies feeling tight, tired, and stuck. Yoga focuses on whole-body movement and awareness. Yoga poses can improve flexibility, build strength, release chronic tight muscles, and increase mobility.

Lowers Your Risk of Heart Disease

Yoga has been shown to lower high blood pressure and cholesterol, and protect your heart.[26] Studies have found that yoga is just as effective on your cardiovascular system as walking. There are so many different styles and types of yoga to choose from, and the good news is that you can reduce your heart disease risk simply by being consistent with any form of yoga rather than a specific style.

Helps You Relax and Sleep Better

Studies show that yoga drastically lowers the levels of cortisol in the body, which makes you feel more relaxed. There are several different aspects of yoga. One aspect is getting yourself into a posture, and another is breathing correctly while you practice the pose. The breathing practices you do in yoga play a huge role in releasing stress and calming your nervous system. Restorative yoga is best for deep relaxation and to prepare you for sleep.

Increases Your Creativity

Research suggests that when you regularly practice yoga, you stimulate alpha brain waves (also known as the happy-calm brain waves). I personally refer to my yoga mat as my "idea factory." When my body is tense, tight, or if I am stuck creatively, I head to my yoga mat. I walk off of my mat having entered a meditative moving state and receive plenty of ideas and solutions to any issues I had before practicing.

It Can Be a Moving Meditation and Increase Positivity

If you find it difficult to sit still and get yourself into a meditative state, consider yoga as your moving meditation. The yoga mat can become a place where you go to find your edge, challenge your thoughts, and actively let go. Imagine that you are wringing out any negativity from the body as you practice a twist pose. As long as you bring all of the elements of mindfulness into your practice, setting an intention at the beginning of your class, being present for each pose, and practicing controlled breathing, you can reduce the stress that is contributing to negativity, thus drastically improving your overall mood and helping you achieve a more positive mindset.

Yoga doesn't have to be an hour-long class to get the benefits you're looking for! It's not how long you practice; rather, it's having a consistent, regular practice to reap the benefits. Yoga can be a five-minute sequence in your office chair at work, done in your bed (yes, literally on your mattress) before you go to sleep at night, or on a yoga mat itself.

Although there are many different styles of yoga, there is one sequence that is the gold standard for receiving endless health benefits called "Sun Salutations." If you practice ten rounds of Sun Salutations each day, you will notice massive results in your suppleness, energy levels, and even a stronger back! Here's exactly how to practice this sequence.

Begin by standing at the top of your mat with your feet together. This is the time when you can set an intention for your practice, so bring your hands to prayer, close your eyes, and set an intention such as: the intention to cultivate your personal power, or the intention to bring in softness.

Inhale and lift your arms over your head, lean your hips forward and arch your back.

Exhale and slightly bend your knees as you fold forward, bringing your chest to your thighs.

Inhale and come up halfway to a flat back, placing your hands on your shins.

Exhale and step back into a high plank pose, with your shoulders over your wrists and keeping your back straight.

Continue exhaling and lower halfway down to the ground, keeping your elbows in. For a modified version, do this with your knees touching the ground to support you.

Inhale again. Keeping your legs straight, move the top of your feet to touch the ground as you lift your chest and bend slightly at the waist, using your arms to support you.

Exhale and lift your tailbone, using your core, to come into a downward dog. Keep your back straight and your knees slightly bent.

Inhale, step to the top of your mat, and come into a halfway lift, with a flat back and hands on your shins.

Exhale, bring your feet shoulder-width distance, and come back into a forward fold.

Inhale as you stand up, bringing your hands over your head and arching your back slightly.

End by exhaling and return to your standing pose.

You have just completed one round of a Sun Salutation. Repeat as many times as you'd like!

Gold Movement Trio #3: Weight lifting

The third movement that rounds out this powerful trio is strength training! Lifting weights tones you up, relaxes you, and makes you feel stronger — inside and out! Weight training is important for both men and women, but I want to especially highlight how empowering lifting weights is for women and why it should be included in your movement routine. I personally turned to weight lifting to get back into shape after giving birth. It helped me feel strong and build my strength again. Whatever you do physically will help you emotionally; therefore, as I built more strength in my body with weight lifting, I felt my mind and emotions strengthening as well.

Weight training can sometimes be an intimidating form of exercise if you are brand new to it, mostly because you are unsure of what to do. I assure you that if you lift weights with a plan of what you are going to do ahead of time, you will enjoy it so much more and reap the results you're looking for.

While trying anything new can feel really uncomfortable, it's important to know why weight lifting is so beneficial to your health and well-being. Lifting weights helps you build muscle, tones you up, and increases your metabolism. A higher metabolism means you're burning calories all day, even when you're not working out! Your body will continue to burn off fat 24–48 hours after lifting weights (something that doesn't always occur after cardio). Building muscle is important, especially for women as we age, because it makes our bones stronger and denser, and therefore prevents age-related muscle and bone loss. (Physically inactive people lose as much as 3–5 percent of their muscle mass each decade after the age of thirty).[27] Additionally, it increases your self-confidence and uplifts your mood by triggering the release of endorphins and serotonin. It will improve your balance, boost your brainpower, and heighten your overall physical health.

You may be wondering, how often should you lift weights? It's recommended that you do 2–3 strength workouts a week! You can do lighter weights, use your bodyweight, or lift heavy! This is why the gold movement trio includes yoga, walking, and weight training — you need time in between all three to recover, and all three have specific benefits to creating a well-rounded movement routine.

How to Get Started with Weight Lifting

I recommend starting by attending a group weight lifting

class at your local gym or following a training session online. YouTube has many free videos that you can search for! If you are brand new to weight lifting or it's been a while, please remember to take it easy and listen to your body. Start slowly, have great form, and build your way up. The weight itself isn't the only way to see progress — increasing your repetitions are too, so don't feel rushed to jump up in weight too soon.

Become familiar with the basic weight-lifting exercises and focus on one area of the body each lifting session. Do an upper-body workout on Mondays, lower-body workout on Wednesdays, and full-body workout on Fridays, for example.

Basic Weight Lifting Exercises

Arms: Bicep curls, Hammer curls, Tricep presses, Barbell curls

Abs: Weighted bridge, Weighted seated twists, Kettlebell windmill

Back: Overhead pulldowns, Seated machine rows, Bent over rows

Chest: Dumbbell chest presses, Barbell bench presses, Seated bench flys

Legs: Squats, Leg presses, Lunges, Deadlifts

Shoulders: Dumbbell lateral raises, Seated dumbbell shoulder presses, Reverse flys

Outdoor Bodyweight Bench Workout

Head out for a walk where you know there will be a bench

along your path. Once you reach the bench, stop and do this bodyweight workout:

10 Tricep Dips

With your back to the bench and keeping your knees bent, place your hands on the bench (fingers toward your back), slowly bend your elbows to a 90-degree angle, and push back up to straighten them.

10 Step-ups on Each leg

Facing the bench, place one foot on the seat and stand up straight before setting the foot back down on the ground. Repeat on the other foot.

10 Push-ups

Set your hands on the back of the bench, as wide as your shoulders. Bend your elbows and bring your chest toward the bench.

10 Lunges on Each Leg

Facing away from the bench, bring your right foot onto the bench and scoot your left leg forward so that your knee is directly above your ankle. Slowly bend your left knee, coming into a lunge with your back foot elevated on the bench. Repeat on the other side.

Repeat the entire sequence two more times. Finish your movement by completing your walk.

Move Your Body Every Day in Some Way

I am all about being very intentional with my life, and moving my body regularly is one of my greatest intentions. Use the affirmation below every day to set your movement intention and let your body know you aren't messing around!

"Every day, I move my body in some way."

Use this affirmation as your foundation for moving daily, along with the following suggestions.

End the "All or Nothing" Thinking

Resist the urge to fall into the trap of the "all or nothing" thinking when it comes to moving your body (or when it comes to any area of your life, actually). You likely have this kind of thinking if you say things like, "I'll start that program tomorrow." Or, "Monday is the day I'll start!" Or even, "I don't have two hours to drive to the gym/yoga studio today, so guess I can't get my movement in." The key of movement doesn't require you to go to the gym for an hour or even attend an hour-long yoga class downtown — it can be as simple as doing squats and lunges in your pajamas for ten minutes.

Big changes show up when you make small changes in your daily life. You will see results and the changes you desire when you move your body even as little as ten minutes a day. Shorter, regular movement is better than irregular, longer movement. I guarantee you will feel better if you move 10–15 minutes everyday vs. moving for two hours at a time once a week.

Wear Workout Clothes While Working

As a self-employed entrepreneur, I spend a lot of my days wearing my workout clothes while working from home. This way, I am always ready for some kind of workout. Since many of us are working at home more than ever before, take advantage of this! Wear clothes that make it easy for you to be ready for some kind of workout at any moment. If you do not work from home, you can wear workout clothes to bed if you try to do movement in the mornings, or change into them as soon as you get home. Make it a small ritual you keep with yourself!

Make Movement a Part of Your Morning Routine

Moving our bodies in the morning wakes us up and sets the tone for having a productive and fun day ahead! I highly encourage you to consider adding some form of movement into your morning before you start your day. This doesn't have to be an official workout (unless you want it to be...you choose!), but mostly an opportunity to take care of yourself and your body by simply moving it in a way that feels good to you. Stretch, do five Sun Salutations, lift weights, head outside for a walk — anything goes!

Plan Ahead and Use Your Calendar

Open your calendar for the upcoming week and document the movements you're committed to doing! Studies show that we are more likely to do something when we write it down. Try doing this as part of your Sunday weekly planning, and then keep the dedication to your calendar by moving your body.

Want to make things even more exciting? Ask a friend, co-worker, or family member to join you in your next movement adventure! Yoga together at the lake next weekend? Checking out the new Pilates studio downtown? Heading out for a walk together during your lunch break? Decide on your movement, write it in your calendar, and remember that you're worth keeping your commitments to yourself!

Weekly Movement Schedule Example

Sun	Mon	Tues	Weds	Thurs	Fri	Sat
Trail Walk or Run	Upper Body Weight Training	Chair Yoga at Work	Lower Body Weight Training	Trail Walk or Run	Family Walk After Dinner	Group Yoga Class at the Lake

14 Mini-Movements You Can Do During Busy Days

What you are aiming to do is to simply move more. Understanding that life happens and sometimes we are in a season where a formal workout won't happen as regularly as we'd like, there are ways to incorporate moving our body throughout our busy days! This can look like:

1. Having a dance party! Turn on some of your favorite tunes while you're tidying up or doing the dishes and dance — solo or as a family!

2. Standing up from your desk every hour for 1–2 minutes. Take two minutes and walk around, do some lunges or a couple of Sun Salutations.

3. Doing some squats while you brush your teeth or blow dry your hair.

4. Walking your dog with your partner and catching up on your days.

5. Keeping an exercise ball in your living room and using it while you're watching TV (sit on it, do sit-ups or lunges).

6. Practicing yoga poses, stretching, or doing planks while watching TV.

7. Actively playing with your kids outside! Are they playing tag together? Join them!

8. Practicing calf raises while waiting in line at a store.

9. Practicing some chair yoga poses in between calls or tasks when working.

10. Engaging your core while you're working on the computer or waiting on someone! This feels like tightening your abs and pulling your belly button back into your spine.

11. Parking in the spot that's farther away (this will make sure you walk more).

12. If you are traveling, practice a few yoga poses (or do squats and lunges) during layovers.

13. Practicing handstands in the kitchen while waiting for your veggies to cook on the stove.

14. Doing cartwheels in the grass outside! Have more fun!

Try incorporating a new movement into your busy schedule everyday for the next week. Remember every little shift adds up to the big changes.

A Summary of How to Unlock The Gold Key of Movement

- Be willing to move your body for the sake of feeling good and to celebrate what your body can do.

- Practice the Gold Movement Trio — yoga, walking, and weight lifting — to have a balanced variety of cardio, strength, and stretching.

- Decide on the workouts or exercises you're going to do at the beginning of the week, and put them in your calendar!

- Make this your daily mantra: I move my body every day in some way.

- Start to see regular movement as no big deal and a natural part of who you are.

Affirmations for the Gold Key of Movement

- I always find the time to move my body. I am worth feeling good!

- My daily exercise is perfect for me.

- My daily movement revitalizes me, inside and out.

- I look forward to the time in my day when I get to move just for me.

- I enjoy moving my body to celebrate what my body can do.

- I am completely in tune with my body.

- I am dedicated to building a stronger body.

- I am proud of myself for exercising regularly.

- I release the idea that I have to do all or nothing when it comes to moving my body — I know that every minute I move adds up!

- I have fun moving my body and choose exercises that feel like play.

Turn Your Movement into G.O.L.D.

Grab your journal and use these prompts to reflect on your next steps for unlocking this key:

G: What's **going well** with your movement?

O: What **obstacles** are you facing with your movement?

_____

_____

_____

_____

L: What are you **learning** about movement from this chapter?

_____

_____

_____

_____

D: What will you **do** next to move more, based on what you learned?

_____

_____

_____

_____

Now that you have changed your mind around movement and identified new ways to make moving fun again, it's time to explore the power of nature and all of the healing benefits Earth has to offer to you.

"Rest is not idleness, and to lie sometimes on the grass under trees on a summer's day, listening to the murmur of the water, or watching the clouds float across the sky, is by no means a waste of time."
— John Lubbock

"The goal of life is to make your heartbeat match with the beat of the universe, to match your nature with nature"
— Joseph Campbell

"Look deep into nature and you will understand everything."
— Albert Einstein

CHAPTER 4

The Fourth Key: Nature

The gold key of nature is the practice of immersing oneself in nature through all the senses.

Nature is always supporting you and helping you to expand your inner awareness. It fills you up, grounds you, connects you to your spirit, heals your body, deepens your relationships, and makes you feel alive. It provides you with the solutions you're seeking and helps you to remember that you are a part of everything around you. But deep down, you already know this.

We have all had an experience where nature was all that we needed to feel better, loved, and supported. As you're reading this, imagine a time in your life when this occurred. Perhaps it's been while walking the beach with your toes in the ocean, admiring the trees on a wooded trail, breathing in the fresh mountain air, sitting by a creek and gently touching the moving water, or swimming in a waterfall. Have you ever wondered why you feel so much better after these outdoor experiences?

I had moved 600 miles away from home with my brand-new

husband when I unlocked the key of nature for myself. My husband would go to work at his new job while I was having a hard time finding a job fresh out of graduate school. To pass the time, I started regularly walking a nearby wooded trail named Quail Hollow Park. Sometimes I would walk slowly in silence and take in the beauty of the trees. Other times, I'd blast some music in my headphones and run the trails when I needed to release pent-up anger and frustration.

Looking back at this time in my life, I was going through my own "dark night of the soul," and nature was supporting me through it. It was healing me. It was holding me up when I was experiencing a trying and transitional time in my life.

I remember walking in the woods at the first sign of spring. Pops of green and new life were beginning to sprout all around me. I felt at ease being among the abundance of green leaves, flowers, and plants in the hot summer. I noticed I could more easily let go of my anxieties when I walked on the crunchy leaves in the middle of fall. I would bask in the stunning silence in the deep of winter. No matter how I felt prior to walking on the trail, I would always leave it feeling infinitely better.

The more time I spent walking in the woods and being outside, the safer I felt to follow through with the guidance I was receiving from deep within. Around this time, I started my healthy living blog and began writing about the very topics I am sharing in this book. I soon found myself studying to become a yoga teacher, leading wellness workshops, coaching private clients, and leading others to improve their own health and well-being. And here we are, now publishing my first book. Fulfilling my own unique soul's purpose.

What I'm about to share with you in this chapter has the potential to help you live to your full potential and purpose. Being in nature fills you up with so much good energy that you are then able to go out into the world and radiate creativity and express your own unique purpose. Being in nature also optimizes your health and well-being, and it gives your soul a foundation of safety, so you can go into the world and shine like gold.

Nature Deficit Disorder

Even though we have more technological advances than ever before, people are unhappier than ever. Studies show that the average American spends a total of 93 percent of their lives indoors (87 percent inside buildings and 6 percent in cars). That's just 7 percent of your entire life spent being outdoors![28]

Never before in history have we been so out of touch with the natural world. Richard Louv, author of *The Last Child In The Woods*, published extensive research explaining the direct link between the lack of nature and childhood trends on the rise, such as obesity, Attention Deficit Disorder (ADD), and depression.[29] He defines the lack of time spent in nature, due in large part to the amount of time spent in front of a screen, as, "Nature Deficit Disorder." He argues that people, especially children, are spending so little time in nature that it is acutely affecting their behavior in negative ways, causing them to have a lack of inner peace and true happiness. This is not okay!

We have become so disconnected from the earth that it's making us sick, stressed, and depressed. Too many people are living their lives primarily between four walls and behind a screen, forgetting that we are nature itself. Nature isn't something that is separate from us, as much as we try to remove it from our lives. When we lose our connection to nature, we lose our connection to ourselves. It is a part of us. The more disconnected we are from nature, the more disconnected we are from peace, health, and joy.

Author John Muir, known as the "Father of National Parks," wrote in his published work *John of the Mountains*, "Most people are on the world, not in it."[30] The solution to combating modern stresses and improving our mood is simple: *spend more time in nature.*

Benefits of Spending Time in Nature

In the past when doctors didn't know what else to do to help their patients, they would prescribe patients to spend two weeks at the ocean to heal. Today, doctors are increasingly prescribing time in nature to help with everything from physical to psychological ailments. Nature affects human well-being in multiple ways. Let's go over some of the most powerful ones.

Nature Regulates the Nervous System

Our nervous system is divided into two parts: sympathetic

and parasympathetic. When the body perceives danger, the sympathetic nervous system activates a stress response, also known as "fight or flight." When we are relaxed and calm, we activate the parasympathetic nervous system, where we "rest and digest" and restore ourselves.

Our modern lives are constantly activating our sympathetic nervous system. We have become so used to a crazy, hectic lifestyle that our nervous systems haven't learned to adapt. Many people don't know how to "turn off" from work and feel guilty if they are not constantly busy or productive. I am sure that you can think of a person who has an inability to be still. We are draining our energy by living in a constant high state of stress and are ignoring the simple keys to regulate ourselves. When your nervous system is out of sync, so are you. An important skill for health and well-being is knowing how to relax and activate the parasympathetic nervous system.

Unlocking the key of nature is one way to activate the parasympathetic nervous system, as it invites us to slow down, be present in our bodies, and use our senses while outside.

Nature Reduces Stress and Lowers Blood Pressure

While it's not surprising that spending time in nature can help you to feel less stressed, studies continue to show this happens because outdoor exposure lowers your levels of cortisol (a stress hormone) and this reduces your blood pressure.[31]

This can explain why when you're feeling stressed or overwhelmed, simply going outside and taking a walk makes you feel better! The problem is most people will go outside and try to walk as fast as possible to "get to the end" of the walk. *How* you walk and spend your time outside is just as important as being outside itself. I encourage you to let yourself be present and notice the nature around you to get the biggest benefits of releasing stress.

Nature Improves Your Immune System

People often think that we get colds and the flu more often in the winter because it's cold out, but that's not true. We get colds and the flu more often in the winter because we are inside more often and exposed to higher concentrations of airborne pollutants, including cold and flu viruses. Recent studies have found that breathing in the compounds that are released into the air — such as terpenes, essential oils, charged ions, pollen, fungi, and bacteria — can boost immune systems.[32]

Nature Helps You Be More Resilient

At every stage in my life that has required resilience, I've always found myself spending more time in nature. The more time I spend walking trails, journaling near a body of water, or meditating under a tree, the more I seem to receive the answers I am looking for. I always feel far less stressed and far more hopeful than I did prior to spending time outside. This is because spending time in nature increases your endorphin levels and dopamine production, which promotes feelings of happiness. Being in nature helps you remember your inner strength and your own ability to rise above life's struggles.

Nature Cultivates a Sense of Awe

Nothing makes you feel more alive than being in total awe of the natural world! Think back to the last time you traveled to a national park or experienced the greatness of nature — you'll likely remember the feelings of joy, wonder, awe, and total magnificence! What would happen if you made it a point to seek out natural wonders more often?

Please don't think you need to travel far to experience awe in nature. You might be surprised how many magnificent places are close to home. I thought that I knew all of the natural places that existed in my hometown, but when I let myself look through new eyes, I noticed all that I hadn't explored! My husband discovered that our hometown is located in "The Driftless Area," a region known as one of the few spots in North America that escaped the glaciers from the last ice age. My father and father-in-law, both born and raised in the area, didn't know that this existed in their own backyard either! You'll be surprised what you can find when you allow yourself to see the natural world with new eyes around you. Nature offers the gift of perspective.

See yourself as an explorer of this planet we get to spend a lifetime on! Everywhere you look provides endless beauty and empowers you to know that you are a part of it too. Connecting with the natural world will help you see with new eyes.

Reflecting on your place in the natural universe can blow your mind.

Make a list of five to ten natural wonders that you want to visit in your life. They can be near you or far away; all that matters is that when you think of visiting them, you feel lit up. Make a plan in your schedule to visit the first place on your list as soon as possible.

Nature Taps into Your Creativity

Our creative juices flow when we are feeling expansiveness. This is why being in the presence of a gorgeous place in nature helps you to feel more open and creative. What a "coincidence" that as I write this, I am driving through Sedona to visit the Grand Canyon. My creative flow is tapped being in the presence of this magnificence.

Nature Helps You Judge Yourself Less

Spending time in nature helps you to remember that you are a gift to the world; you are needed and meant to be here. Spiritual teacher Ram Dass wrote this poem to help release judgment of yourself and enjoy life more with inspiration from the trees:

"When you go out into the woods, and you look at trees, you see all these different trees. And some of them are bent, and some of them are straight, and some of them are evergreens, and some of them are whatever.

And you look at the tree and you allow it. You see why it is the way it is. You sort of understand that it didn't get enough light, and so it turned that way. And you don't get all emotional about it. You just allow it. You appreciate the tree.

The minute you get near humans, you lose all that. And you are constantly saying 'You are too this, or I'm too this.' That judgment mind comes in. And so I practice turning people into trees. Which means appreciating them just the way they are."

Ram Dass[33]

Getting the Most Out of Your Time in Nature

How much time do you need to spend outside each day to receive the full benefits? Surprisingly, it's as little as five minutes. A study in the Journal of Environmental Science and Technology states: "In a meta-analysis of ten studies, they found that getting outside—and moving—for as little as five minutes at a time improved both mood and self-esteem."[34]

However, if you want to *significantly* increase your health and well-being using nature, it's recommended that you spend a minimum of two hours a week in the natural world. If that feels like a lot, remember that doing so is an investment in yourself. There's nothing more valuable than investing in you.

When you spend time outside, it's important that you are present in order to maximize the health benefits it offers you. Going outside but being on your phone the entire time is not the vibe we are aiming for. When you are outside, look at the trees, listen to the birds, and touch the flowers. It's these very sights and sounds that are soothing your nervous system.

There are three methods I am going to share with you that you can use to get the most out of your time outside. These methods have been studied and researched extensively in the past few decades to prove why they are so powerful. The first method is grounding, the second method is called forest bathing, and the third method is exposure to negative ions. Keep an open mind to these methods and let yourself work with the one(s) that you are most drawn to! Remember, this is about creating a lifestyle that lights you up and makes you shine like gold.

Method 1 – Grounding: Reconnecting the Human Body with the Earth's Surface Electrons

Grounding is one of the fastest ways to improve your well-being. Grounding is simply touching the earth with your body in some way, and is sometimes referred to as "Earthing." This means doing things like walking barefoot on the grass and touching or hugging the trees with your bare hands. I am known as the person who is always touching the trees with my fingertips as I walk past them, but it's for an important reason. This practice tends to be falsely accused of being a "woo-woo" technique for healing and well-being, even though it has been studied at length for several decades.

This is how it works. The human body can store electricity and is able to direct the flow of this electricity throughout every single cell in the body. This is important because electricity is required for regulating the nervous system. The earth is charged with electrical energy, so when the human body is touching the ground, the earth is electrically recharging the human body and therefore grounds it. When the human body is grounded, it immediately goes into a healing state and does the following:

- Reduces inflammation and regulates the nervous system

- Boosts the immune system

- Improves your mood

- Balances hormones and cortisol levels[35]

Laura Koniver, MD, author of *The Earth Prescription*, explains in her book that she has not only extensively studied the medical research of grounding, but has prescribed grounding as a practice to nearly every patient she's ever had.[36] Practicing grounding supported her patients seeking medical care for everything from chronic headaches, diabetes, and digestive issues to pain and heart issues.

Another way to think of this concept of grounding is to imagine your body as a cellphone and the earth a charging station. What would happen to your cellphone if you didn't recharge it once the battery died? The same goes for our bodies — except many people stay ungrounded and do not recharge their body with the earth. Physical pain, inflammation, discomfort, and other issues can be supported through the earth's healing energy. The earth's surface is the charging station to your well-being!

How to Ground

When one cell of your body is grounded, the entire body is grounded! Meaning the second you make direct contact with the earth, your entire body is instantly grounded. To get grounded, all you need to do is touch the earth with one part of your body.

This looks like touching tree bark as you walk past it, touching a flower in the garden, touching a rock that's on the earth, walking barefoot on grass or sand, or touching the lake with your fingers while riding on a boat.

What IS NOT Grounded

It's just as important to know what is not grounding you as it is to know what is grounding you.

1. Dead tree bark

2. Decks or patios

3. Asphalt

4. Wearing shoes and being outside

5. Walking outside but not having any direct contact with the earth

6. Indoor plants or flowers that have been cut and put in a pot

What IS Grounded

1. Concrete (this means sidewalks and most driveways!)

2. Any flower, plant, or rock that is growing or connected to the earth

3. Trees, bark, leaves

4. Animals who are grounded

5. Oceans, lakes, ponds, and creeks

Ways to Ground During the Seasons

Just as we shared that mother nature provides us with what we need in each season with our food, there are equal opportunities to ground with her during each season as well. Here are some ideas to help you get started with a regular grounding practice year-round:

SPRING

Take your work and meals outside

When the weather becomes warmer and the sun is teasing you to join it, bring your work and meals outside. Work on emails with your laptop barefoot on the sidewalk. Sit on the grass while you're taking a work call. Eat your lunch picnic style outside.

Gardening

So long as you are working with soil that is connected to the earth, you are grounded while working on your garden. This can be a vegetable, flower, or plant garden. Remember, potted plants inside aren't grounded (the soil is no longer touching the earth), so it's important that it's outside on the ground. Bare hands are best, but if you love your gardening gloves, garden barefoot!

Family walk after dinner

This is a fantastic habit to get into! Not only will you be grounded (as long as you are either barefoot or touching tree barks as you walk), but you will also be moving your body to support better digestion after a meal.

Bird watching

Believe it or not, a recent study found that happiness is correlated with local bird diversity. In fact, a 10 percent increase in exposure to birdsong increases happiness to a similar magnitude as a 10 percent increase in your income does![37] You can watch and listen to the birds while you're grounding. Let's make bird watching cool again!

SUMMER

Grounding with outdoor yoga

Moving your body is vital to your well-being, as we discussed earlier, so moving your body while you're grounded outside is combining two healing modalities at once! Just make sure your fingers or toes touch the earth as you're flowing through your yoga poses.

Walk barefoot in your yard daily

Summer gives us long days and warm weather, so walking barefoot should become the norm for you. Whenever you step outside (onto your yard or concrete sidewalk), stay barefoot. You can find me barefoot all summer long.

Ground with the morning sun

Just ten minutes of direct sunlight gives you nearly all of the daily vitamin D you need, which helps to improve your mood and lower your anxiety.[38] Head outside with your morning cup of coffee in hand and let the sun touch your bare skin as you sip and welcome the day. Even one minute can make a profound difference!

Lie on the ground wearing headphones

Relax outside with a playlist, podcast or audiobook and lie on the ground. This could be at your favorite park with a view or under a tree you love — get grounded and relax at the same time.

FALL

Create a nature shrine table

Bring the outside in for your fall decor! Head outside for a nature walk, looking for treasures to place around your home as you explore. Take home with you some items you find: leaves, rocks, flowers, interesting sticks, branches, etc. When you walk past this table at home, it will remind you to go outside and ground.

Ground and let go with a bonfire ceremony

Sit around a bonfire, barefoot, as you journal and list out what you intend to let go and release. When you're ready, set the intention to let go and toss the paper into the fire. (For more on how to set intentions, refer to the key of intention.)

Spend an afternoon walking a wooded trail to admire the fall leaves

Head out to your favorite wooded trail bundled up with your fingertips exposed (you can find gloves that have open fingers). Admire the beauty of the changing leaves, touching the trees as you pass them.

WINTER

Touching trees with your bare hands

If you have a tree in your yard, bundle up to head outside and touch it while you take several deep breaths.

Snowshoe (or go for a winter walk)

Winter tends to keep us hunkered inside and warm so we are away from the cold. It may be colder outside, but we can still enjoy its beauty and ground for shorter periods of time! Go snowshoeing on a favorite trail, or walk on the shoveled roads — taking a glove off every so often to touch the earth.

Ground on the concrete in your basement or garage

The concrete in basements is typically grounded! This is good news and an easy way to connect with the earth in the cold months without going officially outside. Stand barefoot on the concrete while you fold laundry.

Method 2 – Forest Bathing: Taking in the Forest Atmosphere

Have you ever wondered why the healthiest people you know also coincidentally spend a lot of time outdoors? It's hard to describe the feeling after spending time in the woods, but we know that when we leave we feel healthier and happier. The name for the experience of well-being in nature is "shin-rin-yoku" or "forest bathing," and it originated from Japan in the 1980s. The world's foremost expert in forest medicine, Dr. Qin Li, lists the powerful benefits of this practice in his book, *Forest Bathing: How Trees Can Help You Find Health and Happiness.*[39]

- Reduces stress, anxiety, depression and anger

- Increases energy, creativity, concentration, and memory

- Improves sleep

- Boosts the immune system

- Improves cardiovascular and metabolic health

- Induces psychologically calming effects

- Boosts the amount of your natural killer cells (NK cells)[40]

When we are in the forest, our five senses — sight, smell, sound, taste and touch — are heavily impacted and contribute to our well-being. Forest bathing is slowly walking through the forest while taking in the atmosphere using all five of our senses.

Greatest Benefits Are in the Air

You know that "clean tree air" you breathe in when you're surrounded by trees? That is quite literally plant medicine that you are inhaling. The greatest effect of forest bathing is in the tree scents, because trees release their scents into the air from natural oils called phytoncides. The main components of phytoncides are terpenes, the aromatic compounds that give plants their smell. Not only does the air in the forest have a higher concentration of oxygen and phytoncides, but it also contains microbes — a "good" bacteria that interacts with our bodies to boost our immune system and make us feel happier.

If you can't get out into the forest on a regular basis, diffusing pure essential oils is another way that you can breathe in terpenes and get similar benefits. This is why exposure to pure essential oils is known to have a profound effect on your well-being. I personally diffuse oils in my home two to three times every day for this very reason. Just make sure that you are diffusing good-quality essential oils in order to truly access the terpenes. Here are some beautiful forest blends to try:

FOREST MEDITATION
3 Douglas Fir
3 Tangerine

MORNING TREES
5 Lime
2 Siberian Fir

HAPPY HOME
3 Arborvitae
2 Sandalwood
2 Wild Orange

SWEET SUNSET
3 Lime
2 Bergamot
2 Arborvitae

How to Do Forest Bathing

It's simple to connect with the trees and bathe in the forest. What is most important is being mindful as you engage all of your senses. There are certified forest bathing classes that you can attend, or you can follow these steps and host your own bath in the woods.

Choose a Location

The first step is to choose a green area — and this doesn't have to necessarily be a densely forested area! Think areas like: a local park, a trail through a neighborhood, or a nature preserve. Let your intuition guide you to the right trail, shaded area, or bench on your path!

Slow Down

This is a very intimate and reflective experience, so please be sure to take your time and slow down when forest bathing. Silence your phone. Decide how long you will stay in the woods for this experience. If you're going with someone else, create a rule that everyone will stay quiet until you're finished. Walk on the earth like each step is a prayer. Be gentle with your movements. Notice how "nature doesn't hurry, yet everything is accomplished" (a famous quote by Chinese Philosopher Lao Tzu). Align your energy with the energy of nature.

Engage All Five Senses

Allow the forest to play on all five of your senses. Breathe in the healing aroma of the trees with each breath. Gently touch the bark and the roots of the trees. Taste the flavor of the forest as you slowly walk through its magnificence. Listen to the wildlife living in the trees and the leaves ruffling in the wind. Listen to the sound of crackling twigs as you walk on the earth. Take in the sight of the trees as if it's the first time you're seeing them. Allow the forest to unlock better health, release your stress, and fill you up with calm energy.

Play (Try Different Activities)

- Stop at a bench or tree stump to meditate.

- Make a heart on the ground with any rocks, twigs, leaves or branches you find.

- Practice yoga or any other form of movement.

- Journal or write a poem with the trees surrounding you.

- Study the plants (download an app on your phone that identifies plants for you to learn).

- Camp! Bring a tent and a cooler of food and spend the weekend in the woods.

- Is there a creek or lake in the middle of the wooded area? Try your forest bathing experience while kayaking!

- Explore new wooded trails and treat it like a new adventure.

Enjoy the Quiet

Not only will you enjoy healing and the quiet when you're forest bathing, but you will also be getting away from the noise, the constant "go go go" and daily life stressors. Allow nature to wrap you up in a feeling of calm energy. As she holds you in her silence, know that this allows you to remember that you're a part of the larger whole, which often can help us to think more of others.

The Japanese scientists studying the effects of forest bathing found that going on a forest bathing trip once a month offers mind and body effects that last as long as thirty days.

Method 3 – Exposure to Negative Ions

If you're a "water person" and were hoping that water would be a healing method to unlock the key of nature, you're in luck! Negative ions are charged molecules that float in the atmosphere and are found near bodies of water. When we are exposed to high amounts of negative ions, studies show that our mood and well-being are directly impacted.

Scientists say that high levels of negative ions are generated in large quantities of water, and are found in forested, wooded areas, bodies of water like lakes, waterfalls, oceans, and after thunderstorms! Experts say that negative ion exposure increases our levels of serotonin (a key hormone that stabilizes our feelings of well-being and happiness), helping to relieve stress and alleviate depression.[41] This could be another reason why nature is so healing for us — exposure to negative ions may improve our own mindsets.

How to Increase Your Exposure to Negative Ions

Remember, negative ions are generated from moving water and in wooded areas, so the best option for increasing your exposure is to spend time in nature. We've already shared plenty of methods to be in the forest, so here are some ideas for how to increase your exposure to negative ions:

- Play in the rain.

- Go for a hike near a creek, follow a trail to a hidden waterfall, or find a beach and walk near (or in!) the waves.

- Thunderstorms outside? Perfect! Wait for the lightning to pass and take a walk outside.

- Open your windows after a rainstorm to let in some fresh air.

- Move your body near water, such as by practicing yoga at the beach.

What If You Don't Have Access to a Forest or Park?

While I encourage you to seek out trips to leave the city if you don't have access to nature, you can always supplement by bringing nature into your home. The more often you're surrounded by nature, the better!

- Have a few living houseplants in your home or office.

- Keep your window coverings open to allow light in and open the windows often to allow in the fresh air.

- Plant trees in your neighborhood.

- Join a community garden.

- Find any pockets or areas of grass to take a work call, write in your journal, or have lunch or dinner!

- Keep photos or artwork of nature throughout your home and on the background of your phone and computer. Even looking at pictures of nature can reduce stress.

- Regularly diffuse essential oils.

- Research local natural wonders that you'd like to see and add them to your calendar to make a trip.

- Walk outside as much as possible — getting any outdoor air, even in urban areas, is better than staying inside too often.

A Summary of How to Unlock the Gold Key of Nature

1. Heal your Nature Deficit Disorder by spending at least five minutes a day outside.

2. Ground every day in some way and practice different grounding techniques depending on the season you are in.

3. Incorporate one forest bathing session per month into your life to regulate your nervous system.

4. Bring nature inside of your home. Have real plants in your office, hang pictures of nature, and open your windows regularly.

5. If you can't go outside among the trees, you can diffuse pure essential oils to connect to nature through your sense of smell and remind you of the peace and quiet of the forest.

Affirmations for the Gold Key of Nature

- I honor that nature nurtures me in mind, body, and soul.

- It feels good (and I deserve) to spend time outside.

- I am deeply grateful to be living on this beautiful planet.

- I choose to reignite my sense of curiosity and awe of the earth.

- I am impressed that the trees remind me to release judgment of myself and others.

- I easily find balance and live at the pace of nature.

- I choose to slow down and regulate my nervous system with the help of the earth.

- I flow through the seasons of my life just like nature does.

- I walk on the earth barefoot, with each step a prayer of gratitude.

Turn Your Nature Time into G.O.L.D.

Grab your journal and use these prompts to reflect on your next steps for unlocking this key:

G: What's **going well** with your time in nature?

O: What **obstacles** are you facing getting into nature?

_____

_____

_____

_____

L: What did you **learn** about nature from this chapter?

_____

_____

_____

_____

D: What will you **do** next to get into nature more?

_____

_____

_____

_____

If you want to dive deeper into the concepts of this chapter, here are some recommended books:

- *The Earth Prescription* by Laura Koniver, MD

- *Last Child In The Woods* by Richard Louv

- *Forest Bathing: How Trees Can Help You Find Health and Happiness* by Dr. Qing Li

You've now discovered the healing key of nature — why it's imperative to spend time outdoors to reduce your stress, enhance your health, and exactly how to start doing it. Remember, you are a part of nature. It is about going outside to go within, and the more you do so, the more you'll benefit from it! Simply being outside is making you healthier, happier, and more resilient.

In the next chapter, we are going to discuss the key of mindfulness, which is the practice of being in the present moment. It's time to learn exactly how to be here now.

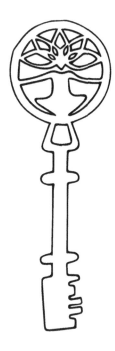

"Mindfulness gives you the inner space and quietness that allow you to look deeply, to find out who you are and what you want to do with your life."
– Thich Nhat Hanh

"Life is not a journey you want to make on autopilot."
– Paula Rinehart

"To be calm is the highest achievement of the self."
– Zen Proverb

CHAPTER 5

The Fifth Key: Mindfulness

The gold key of mindfulness is the practice of increasing one's awareness of the present moment.

Mindfulness has received a lot of attention in recent years, but it is not a new concept by any stretch of the imagination. Mindfulness has roots in the East and dates back around 2500 years. The concepts of mindfulness were brought to the West in the 1970s. Today, more people than ever are seeking the wisdom that mindfulness can provide, but they aren't sure how to apply it. This chapter will help you identify practices that will be the most useful for you and your life. No matter who you are or what your daily life is like, there is a mindfulness practice that is perfect for you.

When I was dating my husband during college, his brother gave me the hilarious and unfortunate nickname "Crank Dog." This nickname implied that I was constantly "cranked" or upset about something. I was anxious all of the time and it showed up as me needing to be in control and needing for things to go my way. Anxiety often shows up when the majority of your thoughts are focused on the future, which is a place that is not here and technically doesn't exist yet.

What happened, though, was once things went my way and I felt like I had control over something, then I'd find something else to feel anxious or "cranked" about. The cycle never ended. On my own journey of well-being, I started realizing that I was wasting my precious time and energy trying to be in control. What I really wanted was to be joyful and happy. The Dalai Lama says, "The purpose of our lives is to be happy,"[42] and you can't be happy when you're not present or always wishing something were different.

So, how did I transform from Crank Dog to Zen Babe? Mindfulness. I learned how to train my mind to come home to myself. I learned that the ultimate gold key is within me, and that everything I was trying to seek, find, and become was already there. I realized that I held the key to unlock my own best self and that it had been there all along. This is true for you, too.

I've learned how to release control and anxiety and embrace the magic of being and enjoying my life. To put it simply, I discovered how to let myself be joyful and happy. One of the most influential spiritual teachers in the world, Sadhguru, often says in his interviews that there aren't good or bad people; there's only joyful or miserable people.[43] And as I've mentioned, I believe that the world needs more happy people.

This is your life, and your job is to be awake, aware, and present for it. Constantly waiting for the weekend, waiting for the next hour, or waiting for something else to arrive is not mindfulness. When you're mindful, you are not wishing you were somewhere else or feeling a different way. Instead, you are embracing the moment with arms wide open. It's about being right here, right now because "we have only now, only this single eternal moment opening and unfolding before us, day and night," as author and mindfulness expert Jack Kornfield says.[44]

What is Mindfulness?

Research shows that 47 percent of people spend *almost all of their time* thinking about something other than what they are doing.[45] Unfortunately, doing this is exactly what kills your happiness! Learning to be mindful is the practice of paying attention to what's happening inside and outside of you in the present moment. Mindfulness is having an accepting and kind attitude toward yourself and the present moment. It's about training your mind and body to be in the now, which is an essential skill to improve your health and well-being. Time is our most valuable currency, and when it's gone, it's gone. It's in your best interest to experience each moment to its fullest, so you won't miss anything in your life.

One of the first ways I learned about mindfulness was the analogy of doing the dishes. It was so simple, yet so profound and life-changing for me that I want to share it with you now. Think back to the last time you did the dishes, an everyday, mundane task, and ask yourself what you were thinking about. Were you thinking about the conversation you had earlier?

Were you thinking about a work task that was heavy on your mind?

Spiritual leader and author Thich Naht Hahn wrote in his book, *How to Eat*, that, "The idea that doing dishes is unpleasant can occur to us only when we are not doing them. Once we're standing in front of the sink with our sleeves rolled up and our hands in warm water, it's really not bad at all."[46] Try being mindful the next time you do the dishes. Notice how the warm water feels on your bare hands. Smell the natural aroma of the non-toxic dish soap you're using. Look at the color of the dishes, notice how you are placing them in the dishwasher. Feel the floor under your feet as you stand over the kitchen sink. This is about noticing the things that are right in front of you.

Your breath happens twenty-four hours a day, but how often do you notice it? Many people have a false belief that they are present for their life when they are not. Just because your body is doing something does not mean your mind, and therefore your awareness, is there for it. We are so used to running around from thing to thing while thinking about the next thing that we aren't even present for the current thing! Then we say, "I just wish it were spring," or, "Wow, that weekend went by so quickly." The secret to a happier life is to be fully present in your life, from minute to minute.

Mindfulness is a subtle shift in the way you are being, which you can learn to do without the underlying feeling of rushing. It is about opening your heart and accepting the present moment. The goal is to get your mind, your body, and your heart all in the same place at the same time. For example, as you are reading this book, simply be reading the book. You probably have a million other things you could be doing right now, but giving yourself this time to settle into the current moment while being fully present will bring you the joy and calm you are seeking.

I don't have regrets that time is moving too quickly or that seasons fly by because I am adamantly present for each moment. I soak in the moments, for I know that the little moments are really the big moments. The present is the only time this moment will ever exist exactly as it is. I don't take it for granted; I relish in the moment. When things get crazy in life, the key is to mindfully take it one day, one hour, one minute, and one breath at a time. When you are fully present for your life — both the pleasant and the unpleasant moments — time doesn't seem to go as quickly.

Life is so much more fulfilling when you're fully in each moment! Treating each moment as special, each day as a gift, each step you take as sacred, each hug you give a loved one as the most beautiful hug, and each cup of coffee you make as the best cup of coffee you've ever made is how you unlock the key of mindfulness.

Your life doesn't exist in the past anymore; that past is over. Your life doesn't exist in the future; that isn't here (and might never be). Your life only exists right here, right now. Do you want to be happy? Then let yourself be here now. Be in it during the mundane and everyday moments, because those are massive moments. Be in it during the exciting, exhilarating moments, because those are massive moments. Be in it during the hard, sad, frustrating, disappointing moments, because those are massive moments.

Accept this moment. Surrender to what's right in front of you. This is your life. Right now. Let each moment reveal itself as the miracle that it is. Life can be simple and easy if we let it, and it can start with something as painless as showing up to do the dishes.

Living Life on Autopilot

An easy way to distract ourselves from the present moment is to live life on autopilot. Living on autopilot feels like picking up your phone with an intention to complete something, but thirty minutes later, finding yourself scrolling and wondering what you were doing in the first place.

Here are some examples of living on autopilot, and how to turn these moments into mindful gold.

AUTOPILOT	MINDFUL
You multitask	You focus on one task at a time
You rush through the day in reaction mode	You flow through the day with gentle awareness and focus
You take life's pleasures for granted	You enjoy life's pleasures
You have a limited mindset	You have a growth mindset of openness and curiosity
You do things without thinking	You do things with a calm awareness
Your thoughts are primarily re-living the past or projecting into the future	Your thoughts are primarily on the present moment
You miss the details	You notice the details
You overthink and overanalyze	You make decisions quickly and commit
You aren't clear about what's important to you	You know what is important to you and act accordingly
Your days are like the day before	You change your daily routine with intention
You don't really know yourself	You know who you are

If you are living your life on autopilot and desire a course correction, mindfulness is the answer. At the most basic level, the word mindful means "to remember." We have constant streams of information coming at us throughout our day, from emails, to text messages, to social media check-ins, not to mention countless meetings. Everything and everyone wants our attention, and if we aren't mindful, then they will get it. Becoming a mindful person is a skill that requires you to train your brain to be aware of the present and what you are doing now.

How to Move More Mindfully Through Your Life

Building upon what we covered in the key of nutrition, let's use mindful eating as an example for how to move more mindfully in your life. I was attending a silent retreat when I practiced eating a mindful meal that turned into a spiritual experience. The retreat was located in a beautiful place in nature filled with trees, trails, and animals. We were instructed to find a spot in the woods alone and do nothing but mindfully eat our meal.

I ended up on a bench with a view, surrounded by trees and birds. I was silent, still, aware of my surroundings, and without any distractions. I took a slow, mindful bite of a fresh cherry and it felt like I had just tasted a cherry for the first time in my life. Each small bite filled all of my senses, and I can still taste the cherry to this day!

There are some key things you can do to help you experience more mindfulness no matter what you are doing or where you are. This can be done by practicing different ways of just being with the present moment, just as I did that day eating my cherries in the woods. The more you practice these ways of being that I am about to share with you, the more they will become second nature.

Genuine Presence

Bringing a genuine presence to your day will allow you to notice how your inner and outer self feels moment by moment. The more you bring this calm, genuine energy forward into everything you do, the more you cultivate a clear awareness in your mind, which helps the brain from being overloaded.

The more you know yourself, the more mindful you are. Being in tune with your emotions, your thoughts, and your body is a beautiful practice of mindfulness. When you wake up in the morning, ask yourself: How do I feel today? What do I want? What am I grateful for? Reflecting on these beautiful questions each morning, even for a moment, has the power to shift your energy from scattered and rushing into calm and genuine.

Start to see yourself as wearing a coat of light around your body. What color is the coat that you are wearing throughout the day? Is it dark and gloomy? Or is it a bright golden light? Practice wearing a coat of golden light, and bring that light into your presence wherever you go. Even if you don't leave your home or see anyone else, wear the golden light coat just for you.

This is how it feels to bring a genuine presence to your life.

Know that when you are living a happy life, you are spreading that light to everyone around you. Do not be surprised when your friends, your family, and even your community notice the energy you are emitting. Your genuine presence is for the highest good of everyone.

Slow Down and Stop Multitasking

When I am really devoted to a project or a goal, I am all in. I used to think that being all in meant that I had to go, go, go as fast as I could toward the goal or else it wouldn't happen. After years of living in that energy, I was forced to slow down after reaching my limit and hitting burnout. When I slowed down, I had to be mindful of what exactly I was doing. I had to delegate, learn how to say no, allow myself to say yes to the right things, and focus on only what served me and my purpose. I didn't have to do it all myself. I could slow down to speed things up. This is because a mindful mindset is defined by two main skills: focus and awareness.

This is an ongoing practice to master, however. Even as I am writing this book I am finding myself feeling rushed, "behind," and trying to do a million things at once. But this chapter in particular is reminding me that these are just thoughts that I am used to thinking and that they're sabotaging my peace! It's safe for me to enjoy the process of a big project! It's safe for me to slow down even with my to-do list being pages long. I know that when I focus on one thing at a time and without rushing, more gets done.

Dedicate yourself to being a "single-tasker" instead of the common "multi-tasker." Not only does multitasking not work (research shows that multitasking limits our cognitive ability to the equivalent of an eight-year-old doing the task[47]), but when you focus on one task at a time, you are able to get more done. This sounds counterintuitive, but when you slow down, you are able to achieve more. Mindfulness isn't about going in slow motion. It's about stripping away distractions and staying on track to focus on what you said you were going to do.

I urge you to begin thinking about the safety of slowing down. Slow down, do one thing at a time, and go about your life with ease. If you don't do this yourself, then life will eventually force you to do so through illness, pain, and exhaustion.

You are safe. It's safe to breathe. It's safe to do one thing at a time. It's safe to slow down. Your entire life will thank you.

Choose Peace Instead of Anxiety or Stress

Peace is a feeling we all strive for on a daily basis. You have the power to choose to feel at peace instead of anxious or stressed at any moment. Whenever you find yourself in moments of doubt, bring your awareness to those fear-based thoughts and choose to see the situation differently. Author Wayne Dyer taught that when you change the way you look at things, the things you look at change. So, when you want to see a situation through the lens of peace, you can do it in an instant by saying, "I choose to see peace instead of this," as the spiritual text *A Course in Miracles* teaches.[48]

In the book *A New Earth: Awakening to Your Life's Purpose*, author Eckhart Tolle wrote, "If peace is really what you want, then you will choose peace. If peace mattered to you more than anything else and if you truly knew yourself to be spirit rather than a little me, you would remain nonreactive and absolutely alert when confronted with challenging people or situations. You would immediately accept the situation and thus become one with it rather than separate yourself from it. Then out of your alertness would come a response. Who you are (consciousness), not who you think you are (a small me), would be responding. It would be powerful and effective and would make no person or situation into an enemy.

"The world always makes sure that you cannot fool yourself for long about who you really think you are by showing you what truly matters to you. How you react to people and situations, especially when challenges arise, is the best indicator of how deeply you know yourself."[49]

You can also practice saying "peace starts with me" to help you choose peace over stress. In any stressful situation, pause and notice the stress in your body and recognize the thoughts you are thinking. Instead of continuing down the stress spiral, say, "Peace starts with me" repeatedly in your mind until you feel the peace wash over your body.

The Power of Silence

You can't think your way into clarity or calm energy, but you can allow it to come through you in the silence. A lot of us feel the need to figure something out about the future. We obsess over an outcome or an answer, yet this is what quickly takes us out of the present moment. It robs us of living and enjoying our lives right now. The solution to stop obsessively thinking is to embrace silence. Get quiet. Be still. Take a moment to simply be. Embrace the gap and silence in between the doing.

Many of us are afraid of what will come up when we are still and quiet. To avoid this, we do anything we can to distract ourselves: watch TV, doomsday scroll through social media, overbook ourselves in our calendars, schedule every minute of our day, mindlessly shop — the list goes on.

I once held a women's retreat in Sedona and was discussing this with the owner of the retreat center. He suggested that when we are trying to escape the present moment, we should ask ourselves: *What is not enough about this moment that I am trying to compensate for?* When you're aware of the power of the present moment and the magic of stillness during the in-betweens, you unlock the key of mindfulness.

Restful Listening

This is the practice of listening without the need to respond in any way. It is the form of listening that allows you to be fully receptive and open to any answer that arrives. With an open mind, you enter a space where you can create connection to your deepest truth.

Listening to someone to really hear them is different than

listening to someone in order to respond. You are not genuinely listening when you are waiting for someone to finish speaking in order to get your point across. Restful listening is a mindful act that you can practice by being open and present.

Refuse to always want to be heard and "right," and instead give the gift of listening. Your genuine awareness and presence is the state of being that will allow you to be calm and centered while listening. Think about how many relationships would improve if we all genuinely listened to one another without needing to prove or "wait for our turn" to share. Restful listening requires a mindful participant. Do you want to be right, or do you want to be happy?

When someone is sharing or venting to you, be mindful about how you can truly support them. You may even ask them, "Do you want me to just listen right now, or do you want my advice?" You can even ask yourself this same question when you are the one who is sharing or venting.

Spend Time in Nature

Go outside and relax under a tree. Take in Lao-Tzu's reminder: "Nature does not hurry, yet everything gets accomplished."[50] Notice how nature isn't judging you. Nature isn't thinking about the next season; it's not thinking about the storm that passed through. It's right here, in this moment, being.

Nature reminds you to slow down, stay open, and appreciate the beauty that is right in front of you. Simply spending more time in nature will teach you how to be more mindful.

Non-Judgmental Awareness

Another definition of mindfulness is that it is an "intentional, non-judgmental awareness of the present moment." What exactly does the non-judgmental part mean? To me, it's practicing being aware of the present moment without labeling it as "good or bad." It simply just is. Our brains tend to label, interpret, or judge something as right or wrong, fair or unfair, important or unimportant, good or bad, almost instantly. Being mindful asks us to recognize when we are in judgment and instead be curious about our response, without judging ourselves. It's about pausing and getting a new perspective. Was this judgment something that just popped into my head? Is there another way I can see this?

The world went through a heavy time of judgment during the COVID pandemic. People were judging each other for the choices they were making or not making, and it caused an already stressful time to be even more traumatic. This time was an opportunity for us to all release judgment of one another and instead practice non-judgmental awareness. This mindful practice is not easy by any means, especially when emotions are high, but it is simple. To bring mindfulness to life means being alive.

Everyday Tips for Being More Mindful

In his book *How to Eat*, Spiritual Leader Thich Naht Hahn

wrote, "Every minute can be a holy, sacred minute. Where do you seek the spiritual? You seek the spiritual in every ordinary thing that you do every day. Sweeping the floor, watering the vegetables, and washing the dishes become holy and sacred if mindfulness is there. With mindfulness and concentration, everything becomes spiritual." This is how I believe we can be more mindful every day. Here are some more specific tips for doing so:

In Your Home

- Keep the TV off and resist the need to have constant background noise.

- When you are resting on the couch, allow yourself to rest without worrying about cleaning. When you are cleaning the house, bask in the joy that comes from simply cleaning and organizing.

- Keep newspapers, magazines, and anything else that will distract you from your own life out of sight.

- Do your laundry and make the bed. Both are mood-boosting habits that will help you take more responsibility for your own well-being.

- Practice eating mindfully at the table during meals.

In Your Work

- Meditate on your work commute, or if you WFH (work from home), meditate at your desk before you begin any work.

- Do one thing at a time (one tab open at a time, complete one task at a time). Use a post-it to write down the task you are focusing on, and put it on your computer.

- Take several deep belly breaths before a work call or a task that requires deep focus.

- Send notes of gratitude to coworkers or clients whom you are genuinely grateful for.

- Write down three things you're grateful for that happened at work every day before you complete your work day. You will be training yourself to look for the good in your work by doing this practice.

In Your Relationships

- Take a deep breath and a mindful pause before responding with emotion.

- Practice restful listening with your partner. Ask them often, *"Would you like me to listen to you right now or offer you advice?"* and then respect their request.

- Be mindful of your time for each other. If you agreed to be home at a particular time, then be home at that time.

- When you spend quality time with your partner or kids, turn off your phones. Engage in conversation and enjoy that time phone-free and without distractions.

With Yourself

- Create a to-do list.

- Create a not-to-do list.

- Take more breaks. Research shows that taking small breaks throughout the day can help to keep your focus and boost your productivity.

- Be loving and kind to yourself. Remind yourself that you are doing a good job. Talk to yourself like you would talk to your best friend.

- Commit to "turning off" from work when you are not working. Resist the urge to check your emails or social media posts.

- Check in with your emotions, your body, and your mind daily by asking yourself, *What am I feeling, right now?* Then, engage in proactive self-care and stress management based on what you need. Learn to trust yourself.

- Commit to engaging in mindful practices every single day in some way. Journal, meditate, pray, read, breathe — the list is endless.

Mindfulness Practice

Mindful living is a skill that we must learn to develop and nurture, and practicing mindfulness each day will help you cultivate it. When done regularly, these practices will help you unlock the key of mindfulness into your everyday life and increase your health and happiness. The following pages will cover three essential mindfulness practices: the practice of gratitude, the practice of meditation, and the practice of breathwork.

The Practice of Gratitude

Gratitude has the power to change the way you view your entire life and circumstances if you allow it. Gratitude has been scientifically proven to improve your physical health, improve your emotional health, reduce your aggression, enhance your empathy, improve your self-esteem, and reduce your stress. When you are truly grateful you are attracting peace of mind into your life.

Most people think that they are grateful simply because they are. However, if you are not actively practicing feeling these feelings of appreciation, then it's difficult to be grateful when you need it the most. The actual definition of gratitude is the "feeling of thankful appreciation." When it comes to gratitude, you want to be able to feel appreciative when you're saying what you're grateful for. Simply going through the motions of listing out the common "I'm grateful for my family, my friends, and my home" isn't going to invoke the feeling that gratitude brings out in you. So, how do you cultivate the *feeling* of gratitude?

Gratitude is a feeling that needs to be nurtured and practiced. It's not something that comes easily, because our brains are trained to look for what is a threat or what is wrong. When we cultivate gratitude, we are basically rewiring our brains to look for the good that already exists in our lives. This takes practice and repetition.

I once read that if you wrote down ten things you were grateful for every night, then you could change your life after twenty-one days. The only rule was that you couldn't write the same thing down twice. I went all in on this challenge.

I had a beautiful notebook that I wrote in every single night for three weeks straight, and I can absolutely say that it changed my life. By the end of the three weeks, I was writing things down like, "I'm so grateful for my healthy legs because they give me the ability to walk to my job every single day," and I genuinely felt thankful for them! I wasn't writing it just to write it; I felt the gratitude in every single cell in my body.

By cultivating the practice of gratitude, you are upgrading your cells and your entire being. During the day, your mind will begin looking for things that you will end up writing down at night in your journal. Through this, you train your mind to continually seek for things to be grateful for. And the more gratitude you feel, the more you realize that there's always more to be grateful for.

This is an especially important practice during these extremely hard times that we as a society are living through. We are bombarded with headlines and posts of negativity and what is wrong with the world. It takes genuine bravery and courage to step into your heart and ask yourself, "What is going right? What am I truly grateful for?"

Gratitude Journaling

I invite you to do the gratitude journaling challenge yourself, and watch what happens in your energy. Before bed each night, write down ten things you are grateful for. The only rule is you can't write down anything you wrote the days before. Continue for twenty-one days and watch the transformation. It may just show you how to turn your life into gold!

Gratitude Journaling Prompts

If you'd like some help getting started, refer to these gratitude prompts to guide you:

1. Describe one thing you learned today.

2. Describe one thing you love about your personality.

3. Write about a part of the day that you love and why.

4. What is something that is working out for you in life lately?

5. List three people you are grateful for and why you are grateful for them.

6. What do you love about bedtime and why?

7. List three reasons you are happy to be alive right now.

8. What are you looking forward to in the day ahead of you and why?

9. What is your favorite part in your home and why?

10. Describe your favorite foods and why you love them so much.

Daily Gratitude List: Amplify It with "Because"

One of the best ways to help you activate the feeling of gratitude beyond just listing the thing, is to add the word "because" at the end of each thing! Finish each item with "because" to amplify this practice, as the *because* is what helps you activate the feeling and the "why" behind it! Here is what this looks like:

I am grateful for _____ because _____.

Example: I am grateful for my husband <u>because</u> he makes me laugh everyday, he makes me want to be a better human, and we genuinely have a lot of fun together in all of our adventures.

Example: I am grateful for my cast-iron skillets <u>because</u> they are fun to cook with and I know I am using a healthy, non-toxic pan to make meals for my family.

Example: I am grateful for my iPhone <u>because</u> I can work on it, I can create on it, I can connect to my community anywhere in the world from it, and I can capture memories on it.

Gratitude Walk

Being in nature reminds you of the power of now and how to be in this very moment. When you immerse yourself in nature on a regular basis, you'll acknowledge the good in your life more often. Therefore, combining nature with gratitude is a powerful happiness hack. Taking a gratitude walk can help you be present, get happy, and get relief. Gratitude gives you the strength and resilience to process some of the less fun emotions and painful events in life events.

A gratitude walk is mindfully focusing on what you're grateful for as you walk. It can be done anywhere you can walk, but preferably outside. When you go, keep your phone on silent and think about everything you are grateful for in your life. If you are having a hard time thinking of things, let nature do the heavy lifting for you — be grateful for the trees, the birds, the sun shining, and the clean, fresh air. Doing this regularly can nourish your spirit and move stuck energy and emotions through your system.

Movement + gratitude + nature = three powerful *keys* to transformation.

The Gratitude Game

This is a gratitude practice that my husband and I started doing together years ago. The game is simply going back and forth and sharing with each other what you are grateful for. We like to do this during dinner at the table. We will each share one thing we are grateful for and go back and forth at least three times.

Sometimes we will do this in bed before we go to sleep. Not only is it a really fun way to connect with someone, but it deepens your gratitude when you say it out loud. Many people likely do this around the Thanksgiving table, but why are we only doing this game-changing practice once a year? I vote for this being a regular practice, and I am excited to play this game with my daughter as she grows up to teach her the power of gratitude.

The Practice of Meditation

Meditation is a daily mindfulness practice that, if you practice it regularly, can reconstruct your mind and body to be the best version of itself. I've been meditating regularly since 2014, and there's no question it's been the catalyst to unlocking my own potential.

The physical benefits of meditating are truly endless. Meditation can increase your attention span, decrease your back pain, reduce your insomnia, and improve your overall general wellness. Meditation is known to provide the nervous system a rest that is five times deeper than sleep.[51] Another study found that meditation lowers the cortisol levels in the blood, suggesting it can drastically reduce stress.[52]

On a spiritual level, meditation is where you access your true self. You're able to transcend consciousness and allow God (or the universe, spirit, angels, source — whatever word you connect with) to talk to you. Many spiritual leaders often say that "prayer is talking to God and meditation is listening to God." When you meditate you are surrendering your struggles of the mind, which in turn helps you to release judgments of others and walk away from negative situations with love and kindness. Whether you are brand new to meditation or have been practicing for years, here are a few things to remember as you practice.

Begin to See Your Thoughts as Clouds Passing Through

When you are meditating, you are learning to become an observer of the thoughts that are coming through your mind. It is inevitable that you will begin to think of other things when you meditate. Your job is to practice not getting attached to these thoughts or following them in any way. It helps to visualize each thought passing through your mind as a cloud in the sky. Just as the clouds pass through, allow your thoughts to gently move across the mind. Let them pass, and let yourself continue to lie on the grass in peace.

Be the Observer of Your Thoughts

Approach your meditations with curiosity toward the thoughts that are arising. "Huh, it's interesting that that thought just came to mind." Or, "I see that an old memory just made its way in." The more you can observe the thoughts as separate from you, the more deeply you are practicing meditation.

While I am meditating, I see myself "sitting" in the back of my head, watching everything that's happening in front of my head. I separate myself from the mind. This way, you truly become the observer of your thoughts. Many spiritual teachers ask, if you are the observer, who is watching the observer of the observer? Consider using this as a journal prompt the next time you complete a deep meditation session.

Learn How to Detach from Your Thoughts

The act of meditating is the practice of sitting through the thoughts that are coming up without needing to do, engage with, or spiral into the emotion that they bring up. Detach yourself from the thoughts that are coming through. Refuse to allow yourself to feel any way toward the passing thoughts and instead have no meaning or emotion toward them at all. This is easier said than done, especially when you are new to meditation. However, this key — sitting with the present moment and letting the thoughts arise, unbothered and without additional meaning — will set you free.

It's Not About "Emptying the Mind;" It's About "Accessing the Space Between Thoughts"

The goal isn't to "clear your mind" when you meditate. This is often the belief that discourages people from meditating at all. They say "*Oh, I can't sit still long enough to meditate.*" But what they are really saying is that they don't know how to simply sit with all of the thoughts in their mind. If this is you, this tip will help immensely. Instead of trying to empty the mind, let yourself go into the space in between those pesky thoughts. The more you practice, the more you will know what this space is — there is a brief moment of stillness in between those thoughts that come and go. That brief moment in between thoughts is what will provide you with the calm, healing energy you are seeking. Author and MD Deepak Chopra calls this "the gap" or the non-thinking place of your meditation. He says that after meditating regularly long enough, the gap will be so established that the small distractions and passing thoughts will not disturb you as they once did.

Your First Meditation: Start With 3

If you have never meditated before, I encourage you to "start with 3." Find a quiet place where you will be undisturbed, set a timer for three minutes, and sit still with your eyes closed. This may feel like an eternity, and you will absolutely feel uncomfortable. Resist the urge to check the time. Know that your only job is to stay with yourself and all of your thoughts for three minutes. Repeat this daily until you are ready to increase the number to five minutes, and then ten minutes, then fifteen, twenty, twenty-five minutes and so on. Eventually, you will find that a thirty-minute meditation session feels like the same amount of time as the first three minutes you started with on your journey.

Each and every time you meditate, you are accessing the most true and pure part of you. You're allowing space for new ideas, solutions and answers to come through. This is also thought of as receiving "divine downloads," a perfectly timed thought that was *the* solution to your situation. When you meditate you are unlocking your true potential.

GUIDED MEDITATIONS

There are many different styles of meditation. I invite you to explore and discover the style that best supports you. It doesn't matter to me which meditation style you vibe with the most, so long as you meditate regularly. Allow the following meditations to inspire you on this journey. You can choose to meditate first thing in the morning, in the middle of the day when you need a break or a boost, or even to help you fall asleep at night. The best time to meditate is the time when you can fit it in. For guided meditation audios from Alisha, please visit www. alishaleytem.com.

BODY SCAN MEDITATION

This is a great meditation to do when your body is showing signs of stress — your muscles tense up, your heart starts beating fast, your sleep gets disrupted, cortisol surges throughout your body, or your digestion shuts down. In a body scan, you are using your mind to connect with and scan every part of your body, allowing it to relax with ease.

Close your eyes. Either lying down or sitting up, get as comfortable as you can. Bring your awareness to each part of your body, beginning with the top of your head.

Acknowledge how the top of the head feels, and with your exhale, allow yourself to release any tension or stress that you are holding on to in your head.

Bring your awareness to your neck, noticing how the neck feels. With your next exhale, allow yourself to release any tension or stress that you are currently holding on to in your neck.

Bring your awareness to your shoulders and upper back. Notice any tension you're holding on to in your shoulders and upper back. With your next exhale, allow your shoulders and upper back to release the tension and stress that it's carrying.

Continue this meditation, repeating the same sequence with the rest of your body: your arms, your stomach, your lower back, your hips, your legs.

Finish this meditation by bringing awareness to your body as a whole, recognizing how it feels after releasing the stress and tension it's been holding on to.

SHOWER MEDITATION

Before you step into the shower*, set an intention of what you'd like to release and let go of. When you are in the shower, I invite you to visualize the water coming out of the showerhead as bright, white light. Allow this soothing white light of water to wash over your head and body, cleansing it of all thoughts of fear, negativity, and worry. Look down at the drain beneath your feet and notice the water draining these thoughts down. Every cell in your body becomes clean, clear, and vibrant with this cleansing white light washing over it. As you step out of the shower, *notice that you are born again. You have washed away all that you've intended and can now move forward with the protective white light covering you from head to toe.*

*A powerful added step to enhance this meditation is to put a drop of an essential oil on the shower floor, allowing the steam of the water to fill the shower and your senses with its aroma. Eucalyptus, the oil of wellness, is a great oil to use for this practice.

CENTER THE SELF MEDITATION

Close your eyes and take several deep, cleansing breaths. Continue breathing fully and completely until you feel your body begin to relax and be at ease. As you continue to feel more calm, bring your hands into a prayer in front of your heart — your thumbs pressing into the center of your chest. Allow this feeling of being centered and at ease to wash over your body from head to toe. Finish this meditation with several cleansing breaths. When you're ready, open your eyes.

THE GRATITUDE MEDITATION

Close your eyes and take several deep, cleansing breaths. Bring your awareness and focus to your heart space, the center of gratitude and love. Think of someone you are grateful for. Let the image of that person come to your mind, and feel  in your heart the gratitude you have for them. Imagine you are giving them a hug, telling them you love them and are thankful for them in your life. Tell them why you are grateful for them. Let the emotion of gratitude for this person fill up your entire heart space, and spill out into every part of your body. Let yourself fill up completely with your gratitude for this person and smile. Thank you, thank you, thank you. You may repeat this meditation process with other people, situations, places, and things that you are grateful for.

GUIDED MEDITATION TO RELEASE STRESS

Stress is a response that we have to our outer world and events. Let this meditation release stress and bring you into a state of calmness and feeling safe.

Your only job over the next few minutes is to relax your mind to the words of this guided meditation to calm your body and release your stress and tension.

Start by getting into a comfortable position. Once you're comfortable, close your eyes and take a deep, smooth breath in through the nose and a nice, calm relaxing breath out.

Allow yourself to be open to meditation. Inhale fully and exhale completely. As you continue to breathe, let each breath start to get a little deeper, a little slower as you continue to relax your body and find your breath.

As you exhale, relax your shoulders. Try to release tension from your face muscles. Let go of tension in your jaw. As you exhale, let go of tension from the body. Allow this relaxation process in the body to happen naturally with your breath.

Inhale fully and exhale completely. On your next inhale, imagine a warm and comfortable breath filling up your entire body. Exhale, soften every cell in your mind and body.

Now that you're getting the oxygen that you need, realize that your only job right now is to keep yourself as comfortable as possible as the feeling of stress passes.

Fighting against the stress only makes it stronger. Right now, in this moment, just accept that you are feeling stressed.

Let us focus on calming your thoughts to relieve your stress. Repeat the following statements to yourself in your mind: Even though I am feeling stressed, I am okay. This feeling will pass and nothing bad will come to me. I am safe, even though I feel scared. I will be calm soon, even though I am experiencing stress right now.

I will get through this. I am making myself as comfortable as possible, as I wait for the intensity of the stress to decrease. I can help myself to become more calm and relaxed as this feeling passes.

With this peaceful and safe feeling that you've created for yourself, begin to imagine that you're sitting comfortably in a hammock between two palm trees on a beautiful beach. Take in your surroundings — what do you see?

What do you hear on this beach? Notice the beautiful blue water with beautiful clear skies. The breaking of the ocean waves and the sound of birds.

Appreciate all of the beauty that you are surrounded by. You can feel the warmth of the sun radiating through every cell in your body. This is your sacred space. This is the space where there are no expectations.

All is well and you are stress free. Breathe in the warm, calming sun on your skin. Feeling more and more calm and relaxed. As you sit in the hammock, notice where you're still holding onto tension in your body.

On your next inhale, imagine you're sending loving energy to the tension in your body. Allow the warmth of this energy to relax your muscles and release any tension you're holding onto. Inhale love to the tension and exhale out the stress as you release the tension. Continue this process of sending love to this tense area — releasing stress as you exhale.

I easily find calm and peace in my day. Life is simple and easy. I accept myself and create peace in my mind and heart.

As you continue to breathe with the rhythm of peace and relaxation that you have created in this space, remember to know and believe that you are able to connect to this place of calm that you've created at any time.

LET GO MEDITATION

Find a comfortable seat, close your eyes and take a deep breath. Relax your shoulders, release your stomach, let your jaw soften. And with the flow of your natural breath, introduce this simple mantra: on your inhale, repeat to yourself, "Let;" on your exhale, repeat to yourself, "Go." Inhale, let. Exhale, go. Inhale, let. Exhale, go.

Repeat for several minutes, or until you have successfully let go of the emotion of the thing you are holding onto. When you feel a shift in your energy, stop the mantra and gently open your eyes.

Meditate to Benefit Others

I often set the intention that my meditations will benefit the greatest good of all beings. This intention has benefited me greatly, especially during the challenging times we are living in. The truth is that our meditation practice is not just for us. When you are happy and healthy, you are genuinely a better partner, friend, coworker, neighbor, and parent. Declare this intention before you meditate: *May this meditation benefit those I love, those I have difficulties with, and humanity as a whole. May this meditation be for the highest good for all. In liberating my own being, may I benefit others.*

The Practice of Breathwork

When you were a child and you were upset, did your parents ever tell you to "*take a few deep breaths*"? This is because it was helping us to regulate our nervous system and come back into the present moment. The majority of people are chronic shallow breathers. They tend to only use a small portion of their lung capacity when they breathe. In yoga, we refer to the breath as "prana," or life force energy. When we breathe deeply, we are filling ourselves up with life force energy.

When we breathe shallow or take short breaths, we activate our sympathetic nervous system (also known as "fight or flight"), which is where stress, anxiety, fear, and racing thoughts live. Breathwork, or deep breathing in general, is activating the parasympathetic nervous system, which sends a signal to your brain that you are safe and can relax the body and therefore the mind.

Breathwork is a very powerful practice to support you in releasing what is not serving you and hold you into feeling safe, at ease, and present. When we are full of breath, we are full of inspiration. To live your most beautiful, energized life, the breath is essential.

The Basics of Breath

Breathing into the stomach activates the parasympathetic nervous system, which, as we have already covered, is soothing and regulating. Breathing into the chest activates the sympathetic nervous system and is energizing. This can be helpful when needed. However, most people tend to do too much chest breathing, which puts us into an anxious and overwhelmed state. At the same time, breathing too much into the belly regularly can keep us in an overly relaxed state.

Ideally, you are breathing consciously into your belly when you need to relax and consciously into your chest when you need a boost of energy. You want to be able to know how and when to distribute this level of life force (breath) throughout your body. If you focus on a slow exhale, this will help you to calm down. If you want to increase your energy, focus on your inhales, bringing more "life force" into your body. This is why breathwork is such a powerful mindfulness practice: it requires you to be present and aware.

Square Breathing Technique

This breathwork exercise will help you to become centered, improve your heart health, and reduce any anxiety and depression you may be experiencing. It has four main parts: inhale, hold, exhale, hold. Visualize your breath like a square, hence the name of this technique. To begin, start sitting up tall with a straight spine. Inhale for the count of four. Hold your breath for the count of four. Exhale for the count of four. Hold your breath for the count of four. Repeat for several minutes, or until you feel a sense of calm wash over you.

Alternate Nostril Breathing

The benefit of this breathwork exercise is to bring balance to the nervous system. It can quiet the heart, it's both cleansing and calming at the same time, and it aligns both sides of the brain.

To do this exercise, find a comfortable upright position. Close your eyes and take several deep breaths. With your right hand, take your first two fingers (the forefinger and the middle finger, aka the "peace sign fingers"), and place them in between your brows. This leaves your thumb and ring finger available to close the nostril on each side.

Start by closing your right nostril with your thumb, and inhale through your left nostril. At the top of the inhalation, hold your breath as you release the thumb and use your ring finger to close your left nostril. Exhale through the right nostril. Inhale through the right nostril. When you reach a full breath, close your right nostril and open the left. Exhale through the left nostril.

That completes one full round of this practice. Repeat it for 10-20 full cycles. Then rest peacefully in the stillness you created with a relaxed, natural breath.

A Summary of How to Unlock the Gold Key of Mindfulness

1. Refuse to live your life on autopilot and commit to living more mindfully.

2. Bring mindfulness and concentration to every part of your life — your home, your work, your relationships, and within your own heart.

3. Practice feeling grateful to attract peace of mind into your life.

4. Meditate daily so that you can reconstruct your mind and body to being the best version of itself.

5. Live in the breath from moment to moment to live your most beautiful, energized life.

Affirmations for the Gold Key of Mindfulness

- I am centered and calm.

- I find time to be quiet and connect with the power of the pause every day.

- I am grateful for all that I am becoming.

- I allow myself to take things one moment at a time.

- My breath is my anchor.

- Everything in my life is working out for me.

- I am peace; I am love; I am joy.

- Inhale, let. Exhale, go.

- My power is in this present moment. I step into it now.

Turn Your Mindfulness into G.O.L.D.

Grab your journal and use these prompts to reflect on your next steps for unlocking this key:

G: What's **going well** with your mindfulness?

_____

_____

_____

_____

O: What **obstacles** are you facing with your mindfulness?

_____

_____

_____

_____

L: What are you **learning** about mindfulness from this chapter?

_____

_____

_____

_____

D: What will you **do** to be more mindful, based on what you learned?

_____

_____

_____

_____

"If you want to conquer the anxiety of life, live in the moment, life in the breath," as Spiritual Master Amit Ray says.[53] Now that we've unlocked the healing benefits of mindfulness, it's time to explore the power of living with intention. In the next chapter, I will show you how living with intention will improve your mood, your day, and the entire direction of your life.

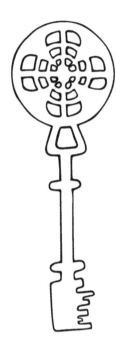

"When you know that you're in charge of your intentions, then
you'll come to know that you're in charge of your entire world."
– Wayne Dyer

"Tell me, what is it you plan to do with your one wild
and precious life?"
– Mary Oliver

"Remember that this is your world. In your world, you can create
anything that you desire." – Bob Ross

CHAPTER 6

The Sixth Key: Intention

The gold key of intention is the practice of thinking, acting, and being with purpose.

Intentions are about aligning yourself with the life that you say you want. How do you intend to live your life? To answer this question, you must first acknowledge and understand just how powerful you really are. Unlocking the key of intention is a thoughtful process that requires you to know yourself, know what you want, and focus your attention on creating it.

When you are intentional with your life, you know what you are creating. You know how you want to spend your days. You know what you want to experience. I'm not talking about overscheduling yourself, or having a strict to-do list each day. I am talking about having a deep inner knowing of who you are and what you want to experience from a deep, soul level. You are in charge of how you design your life. No one but you can create the life that you deeply desire. This is *not* about going with the flow of things; it's about being intentional with your life.

Did you know that everything in your life starts with an intention? Calling a friend, making your morning coffee, or commuting to work all began with the intention before action is taken. You may not have even been aware that you were setting intentions until now. What this means, though, is that you can use intention setting to create a happier and healthier life for yourself when you search within and get honest about what you want. You get to choose how you want to feel!

As a human being, who is well on their way to becoming a well-being, by reading this book, you shouldn't think about where life will take you, but instead about where you want to take life. You have the free will to create the life you want for yourself. Are you using your free will to live with intention? Or are you sitting back and hoping that what you want simply comes to you?

What Is an Intention?

An intention is a guiding principle for how you want to show up in the world. This can guide you at work, at home, in your relationships, or in any area of your life. In order to set intentions, you must know what you value and what is truly important to you.

Think of intentions as the seeds of desire for who we want to be and what we want to feel. We can access these seeds from inside of us when we listen to our soul's deepest needs. It's crucial to acknowledge our desires, because our desires point us to the most fulfilling path we could possibly take. There is a Sanskrit term from yoga philosophy called *sankalpa*, which means that heartfelt desire comes from deep within and has a powerful effect to help you align with your values and make a difference in your life and the lives of others.

Intention setting is about enhancing your life, not "fixing" it. Setting intentions are much more powerful when they are done from a place of feeling whole and enough, not from a place of inadequacy or being flawed. The past doesn't matter when you set intentions. All that matters is where you are going and what you are aiming for. Get excited, because this is a fresh new beginning for your life!

Focus On What You Want

When you choose to live with intention, you are taking charge of your whole world. You can set intentions for how you want to feel the minute you wake up, or intentions for how you will be of service to those who need you. How would your life improve if you put your attention on creating more of your deepest desires? What opportunities would you say yes to? Energy flows where your attention goes.

It's easy for most of us to say what we don't want. It's not so easy to say what we *do* want. The secret to being more intentional is allowing yourself to move toward what you truly want with more aligned thoughts and actions! Resist the urge to say what you don't want, and only focus on what you deeply desire.

Your job is to identify what you want, and then focus on that with your attention. What do you want to expand more of in your life? More love? More money? More travel? More time?

More freedom? Where are you choosing to put your attention? If you aren't quite sure of what you want, you are likely not digging deep enough within to access the answer. You must take the time to disconnect from the outside to go within your heart to unlock this key.

If you find yourself only able to think about what you *don't* want, then you can use that to uncover what you *do* want. For example, let's say you don't want to be stressed. When you focus on not wanting to be stressed, this only creates more stress because you're placing your attention, and therefore your intention, on stress. Instead, think of a new desire, which is typically the opposite of what you don't want. In this example, the opposite of stress is to be at peace. This is now your intention — to feel peaceful.

Danielle Laporte wrote in her book, *The Desire Map*, that "knowing how you actually want to feel is the most potent form of clarity that you can have. Generating those feelings is the most powerfully creative thing you can do in your life."[54] She argues that we must first get clear on how we want to feel within ourselves, and then design our goals and to-do lists accordingly. She says that the question to ask ourselves to find clarity of what we want is: "How do you want to feel?" Give yourself permission to explore your heart's deepest desire.

If you aren't sure of what you want, I will be guiding you through a five-step process to setting powerful intentions in the pages to come. For now, I encourage you to start by setting a simple intention: "*I intend to identify what I want for myself with clarity, ease, and grace.*"

Intentions Are Not Goals

Oftentimes, intentions are confused with goal setting. A goal is a personal need or want, and intentions connect you with your heart's desire. A goal sounds like, "I want to be healthy," and an intention sounds like "Healthy is who I really am." Most traditional goal setting focuses only on the outcome, or on getting what you want. Goals are important to have, but the way we typically go about setting them and achieving them can miss the mark when they aren't supported with an intention.

Goals are a desired result, outcome, or external achievement. Intentions are something you aim for how you want to feel, or the *process* you go through until you get the external achievement. Goals are actions you take, while intentions are the way you live.

Setting intentions on the back of your goals is the secret sauce to achieving them with ease, grace, and focus. This is because you are better able to grow through your actions and learn more about yourself on the journey toward the goal.

Let's say you set the goal to lose ten pounds. How do you think you will feel when you hit that goal? Energized? Now you have your intention — to feel energized every day. Now you can create an affirmation to align with the goal, such as, "I feel energized and happy when I move my body and eat well."

Consider setting your intentions on the back of each goal you have set for yourself. This takes the pressure off and helps you get at what you really want. Feel the difference? Here are some more examples.

GOAL	INTENTION
Go to bed at 10:00 p.m. every night	To be well rested and energized
Publish my first book	To be focused and connected to my truth
Meditate everyday	To be in tune with my feelings and emotions
Lose ten pounds	To feel energized and healthy
Start freelancing	To experience freedom and express my creativity
Earn more money	To experience abundance and overflow in every area of my life

5 Steps to Setting Powerful Intentions

Let me share with you a five-step process to setting intentions that will help you become in charge of your whole world. The five steps are: Get Quiet and Take Time to Think, Articulate and Define Your Intentions, Keep Your Intentions Alive, Release Your

Intentions, and Co-Create Your Intentions with the Universe.

Step 1: Get Quiet and Take Time to Think

Socrates famously once said that "to know thyself is the beginning of all wisdom." If we want to live a more intentional life,
we have to know ourselves better. The way we know ourselves
better is by asking ourselves better questions, as Life Coach
Tony Robbins teaches. When I first started asking myself better
questions, it was an uncomfortable yet exciting exercise to
explore a deeper side of myself. Asking myself better questions
is exactly how I planted seeds of change that helped me to
create and design a life that I love.

There are two critical questions you must ask yourself when
setting intentions: What do I want and how do I want to feel?

Create a Sacred Space

Before you begin the process of setting powerful intentions, I
recommend that you do this in a sacred space. Find a quiet
room where you will be undisturbed.

Gather your materials: a candle, a journal and pen, a warm
blanket, a relaxing playlist of music, something warm to drink,
a cushion or something similar to sit on, and a diffuser with
essential oils. Include anything else that inspires you — such as
a book, incense, affirmation cards, your favorite crystals, etc.

Consider diffusing essential oils to inspire a positive emotive
state while you go through this process. Many essential oils

have relaxing and stress-reducing properties simply by breathing in their plant medicine. Try these blend recipes in a diffuser to support a beautiful state in your room.

INTENTION SETTING	CONSCIOUSLY CONNECTED
2 Frankincense	2 Wild Orange
2 Sandalwood	2 Frankincense
2 Clary Sage	2 Clary Sage
	2 Peppermint
	2 Lavender

Now that you've set the stage with your environment, you will want to begin the process of setting intentions by meditating. Use the following meditation script to help you get quiet and allow your soul to speak to you.

MEDITATION FOR SETTING INTENTIONS

Begin by getting comfortable. You may want to sit or lie down. Close your eyes and take several deep breaths. Continue breathing restfully as you become more and more relaxed.

Bring your attention to your heart space. If you'd like, you can place your hands over your heart. Ask yourself only one question: What do I want?

Then allow any sensations, images, feelings, or thoughts to arise without trying. This is the true meaning of ask and you shall receive. And then...let go.

Do not focus on anything else except repeating the mantra "so hum." So hum is the sanskrit word meaning

"I am," or identifying oneself with the universe. Do this for 10–20 minutes.

Sooner or later, you will have an epiphany, a thought, or something will happen that will give you evidence of what you want. Trust the process.

Once you've meditated, it's time to think. Here are some simple journaling exercises to help you get started with identifying your deepest desires. Grab your journal and spend a few minutes reflecting on the following questions:

1. What do you want more of in your work + life?

2. What do you want to experience?

3. How do you want to feel?

4. What matters most to you?

5. If you could have anything, what would you want?

6. If nobody would be mad at you, what would you want?

7. What are you doing the majority of your day? Do you enjoy it? Does it nurture you?

"The Thriving Five" Exercise

Make a list of five people you admire or look up to. They can be people you know or follow online. Write down the first five people who come to mind. Please do not compare yourself to these people, but rather let yourself be inspired by them!

1. _____

2. _____

3. _____

4. _____

5. _____

Read through your list of people that you admire with curiosity, and for each person write down 1–3 reasons why you
admire their lives. Is it something that they have? Is it their job?
Location? Energy? This is showing you exactly what it is you
want more of in your life! Remember that the light you see
in someone is reflecting your own inner light. If you admire
someone for any reason, you have a part of that light within
you. They are simply reflecting your own inner light to you, and
showing you some of your deepest desires.

Your Values and Time Spent

Make a list of all of the things that are important to you in the
left column. In the right column, make a list of all of the things
that you spend your time doing. Look at the two columns
and see if either of them overlap. Not everything has to align
between the two, but ideally you want most of what you spend
your time doing to align with what's important to you. And if
you find that your lists do not align, try the perfect day exercise
below to help you uncover a more balanced approach.

What Is Important to Me	What I Spend My Time Doing

"The Perfect Day" Exercise

This is a very powerful practice that can help you uncover what it is you want. Many times people will set intentions for what they think they want because it sounds good, but when it comes down to how they spend their days, they realize that is *not* how they want to spend their time.

When you think about what your perfect day could be, you are designing your life! You get to be really intentional with how you want to feel and what you want to experience. Resist the urge to overthink it. Overthinking this exercise can cause you to start projecting an outcome and put enormous pressure on how you think life needs to happen for you. Instead, have fun! This exercise should feel like you are dreaming up your ideal life.

Go through an ideal, perfect day from the minute you wake up until the minute you go to sleep. Think about every single detail — from the home you are in to the sunshine on your face to the smells in your kitchen.

TIME	ACTIVITY
6:00a.m.	e.g.: wake up naturally with the sun
7:00a.m.	
8:00a.m.	
9:00a.m.	
10:00a.m.	
11:00a.m.	
12:00p.m.	
1:00p.m.	
2:00p.m.	
3:00p.m.	
4:00p.m.	
5:00p.m.	
6:00p.m.	
7:00p.m.	
8:00p.m.	
9:00p.m.	
10:00p.m.	
11:00p.m.	

Now that you have taken the time to check in on your deepest desires, step 2 will help you to hone in on how to bring your intention to paper.

Step 2: Articulate and Define Your Intentions

You have reflected and taken the time to dig deep within, and now your next step is to articulate and define your intentions. When we write our intentions down, we make them real; we give them power. Be specific when you write them.The more clear and concise they are, the better. Your intentions are much more powerful when they come from a place of contentment and not from lack or neediness.

I created a wheel that breaks down five significant areas of our life: health and well-being, relationships, career, fun, and your life vision. I call this the Intentional Life Wheel. When you have clear intentions for each of these areas, you create better alignment for living your best life. Here are some examples of what an intention for each area might sound like.

Your Intentional Life Wheel

Health and Well-Being Example:

I intend to live in a healthy, energetic body.

Relationships Example:

I intend to show support and appreciation in my relationships.

Career Example:

I intend to release self-doubt and fully trust myself.

Fun:

I intend to be adventurous and light hearted.

Life Vision:

I intend to move through life with authenticity, achievement, and happiness.

It's your turn. Write out your own intentions for each of the five areas.

Even though I haven't talked a lot about relationships in this book, your relationships are *very* important for your health and well-being! Having healthy relationships reduces stress and is linked to improved overall well-being. To ensure you are enjoying healthy relationships in your life, be intentional about them. Think about the dynamics of your relationships, what you think about them, and how you feel about them. How can you be more intentional with who you surround yourself with and who *you* are in the relationship?

Resist the urge to write down what you believe is "realistic." When you choose your intentions, you are identifying your deepest desires. What you want *is* realistic because you want to feel a certain way and you access that feeling within no matter your external reality. Let yourself dig deep and think big. This process is divinely designing your life.

Write Your Goals for Each Area

At this point in the process, you can write your goals based on your intentions and how you want to feel.

For example, with the health and well-being intention of feeling energetic, you might set a goal to move your body every day in some way. Your intention is to feel energetic, so you might also set a goal to remove anything (including relationships, jobs, and environments) that can be toxic to the body.

If your intention for your life vision is to be authentic and happy, you might set a goal to move to an area that is more authentic to your truth. Maybe your goal is to start a business or a new career direction that feels more authentic to you.

If your intention is to be a supportive and appreciative partner, maybe you set a goal to write your loved one a hand-written note of appreciation every month. Perhaps you set a goal to plan and go on weekly dates together.

The point is that you know the intentions behind each of your goals. The intentions that you've set are from the seeds of desire to how you want to feel and the way that you show up in your day. This is how you intentionally design your life.

Turn Your Intentions into a Vision Board

Once you have your intentions written down, you can create a vision board for them. Vision boards are a way to craft your vision with images in order to sharpen your focus and put your attention toward it.

Be very intentional in the images you choose, because they will very likely show up in your life.

I created the vision board image on this page on New Years Eve 2015. My intention for the upcoming year was to feel adventurous and fearless. I put pictures on my vision board that made me feel adventurous and fearless. I didn't have any attachment to any specific image; I simply appreciated how they made me feel when I looked at them.

A few months after making this vision board, I sold 80 percent of my belongings, packed whatever I could fit in my car, and moved to San Diego, California. I was exploring my new city when I realized while standing at the pier that I had a picture of the view I was looking at on the vision board. You can see the incredible similarities!

Tips for Creating Your Vision Board

Find images or pictures printed out from web pages or magazines that reflect your intentions and how you want to feel. Consider using magazines that you like to read and that contain your interests. For example, if you have an intention to live in your dream location, find travel magazines for that area. Go to your arts and crafts store and find some stickers, fabric, or other items that you are drawn to that will bring your board to life and be a reflection of you. If you prefer, you can create a digital vision board as well.

Take your time, have fun, and make an event out of it. If you rush through the process, you are missing out on the benefits and best parts of the exercise. Truly think about this as an exercise for your soul. When you look at your vision board, you want it to ignite the feelings you are intending to feel!

Once you create your vision board, place it somewhere where you can see it every day. Perhaps in your office or even your closet. You can make the digital version a background on your computer or your phone.

When we look at the images we choose that resonate with us, we are signaling to our brains that this is what we want and this is where we would like to see ourselves. It's a powerful way to engage the subconscious mind and manifestation.

I like to make a vision board for each calendar year, but if you feel called to make one for longer or shorter time frames, please do so. There isn't a right or wrong way to do it, and you can't mess it up. The only mistake you could make after creating your vision board is never looking at it again — instead, you must learn how to keep your intentions alive.

Step 3: Keep Your Intentions Alive

Setting the intention is only the first step. It's up to you to keep your intentions alive by focusing your attention on them. When you put your attention on your intention, you begin to change. A powerful practice for staying connected to your desires and creating a life and feeling that you want is by setting daily intentions.

Commit to Setting Daily Intentions

I take time each morning to reconnect with my soul before going about my day. With this time, I will practice a variety of tools including: setting an intention, meditating, journaling, reading a page from a devotional calendar, or praying. Some mornings I will pull an affirmation card, read a chapter from an inspiring book, or listen to a guided meditation. The routine is different from day to day, but what stays the same is taking a moment to go within.

When you set daily intentions, you set the tone for your day and remind yourself that you are in charge of your life. Mornings are the best time to set intentions for the day ahead. This can be as simple as asking yourself *"How do I want to feel today?"* Having a clear intention at your fingertips can help guide your actions as you move through the day.

If you are brand-new to the practice of setting intentions, you can start with a simple two-minute reflection of how you want to feel. What matters most is that you are creating a foundation to have an intentional day ahead.

How to Set Daily Intentions

Write down in a designated journal each morning the following:

"Today, I intend to _____"

All you have to do is pause and reflect on what you want in the day ahead, and what you'd like to get out of it. Here are some things to think about:

- How do you want to feel today?

- Who do you want to be today?

- What do you need to focus on to achieve your goals?

- What kind of attitude do you want to have today?

- What do you need to commit to today beyond your to-do list?

- What are you most looking forward to today?

Once you've set your intention for the day, reflect on how this relates to your goals. This helps you to get connected to the "why" behind each goal you've set and will set the tone for the day ahead.

10 Ideas for Setting Daily Intentions

Today I intend to:

1. Today I intend to be present in the moment.

2. Today I intend to release self-doubt and negative thoughts.

3. Today I intend to embrace gratitude.

4. Today I intend to choose happiness.

5. Today I intend to commit to the desires within me.

6. Today I intend to laugh and have fun in everything I do.

7. Today I intend to relax and go with the flow.

8. Today I intend to be focused and organized.

9. Today I intend to let divine wisdom lead the way.

10. Today I intend to be open to the limitless possibilities available to me.

Use Affirmations for Your Intentions

Using affirmations to support your intentions is a way to change and transform from the inside out. Once you have your intention for the day, choose an affirmation to align yourself with the intention. Below you will find an affirmation to use with each of the intention examples listed above. Use these affirmations or make up your own to support your intentions throughout your day.

1. Today I intend to be present in the moment.
I live in the present moment and easily release the past.

2. Today I intend to release self-doubt and negative thoughts.
My self-esteem is high because I honor who I am.

3. Today I intend to embrace gratitude.

I express gratitude every day, in every way.

4. Today I intend to choose happiness.

Happiness is a choice I make, and I choose it now.

5. Today I intend to commit to the desires within me.

The universe has my back and supports me in every way.

6. Today I intend to laugh and have fun in everything I do.

Wherever I am, there is laughter and fun.

7. Today I intend to relax and go with the flow.

I easily flow with my ever-changing life.

8. Today I intend to be focused and organized.

I am organized and productive and I love getting my life in order.

9. Today I intend to let divine wisdom lead the way.

Divine wisdom is always guiding me.

10. Today I intend to be open to the limitless possibilities available to me.

I am open to the endless possibilities of this day.

You can refer to the end of each chapter for additional wellness affirmations to find the one you resonate with the most each day.

How to Remember Your Intentions During the Day

- Write your intention and affirmation down where you will

see it. This might be in a journal that you keep on your desk while you're working.

- Write your intention and affirmation on a post-it and put it on your computer screen or stick it to your bathroom mirror.

- Meditate on your intention for a few minutes before you start your day.

- Set an alarm on your phone and in the title of the alarm, write down your intention or affirmation. Schedule the alarm to go off a couple of times throughout the day. When the alarm goes off, take a mindful moment and connect with your intention in your heart.

Step 4: Release Your Intentions

Once you've written down your intentions, let them go. To feel free and surrendered, you must learn to release your attachments. Check in with your intentions frequently, but don't become obsessed with specifics. Let go of any expectations regarding your intentions. Trust that the universe has got your back. Sometimes the universe will deliver you something that gives you the feeling you desire behind your intention, yet it looks different than what you expected.

When you plant a seed in the ground, do you go and dig it back up every day to see how it's growing? Of course not! You water the seed and give it time and space to grow. You trust that it is growing and will sprout at the perfect time. You don't need to dig it up constantly to make sure that it is growing or doing its thing. Your intentions work the same way.

The best way to let go of expectations is by reminding yourself that *"it's this or something better."* Remember, you are after a specific feeling. You don't have to hold on or worry because you can trust that your intentions will show up to support the feeling you deeply desire. You can surrender your intentions with ease. Either it will show up how you imagined, or it will be *even better* than what you imagined!

As long as you are putting your attention toward what you want (like "watering the seed" and removing any weeds that show up around it), then you can relax and trust that they are coming together with ease and grace.

Learn how to embrace not being in control of every aspect of something. Let go of the "all-or-nothing" mentality. Trust that you are moving toward what you want. Know that it doesn't have to be perfect to come together.

Step 5: Co-Create and Manifest with the Universe

You have a powerful energy on your side supporting you every step of the way as you bring your intentions to life. Dr. Wayne Dyer teaches that intention is a field of energy that you can access to co-create the life you desire. This means that the universal energy of pure potential is on your side, if you choose to allow it.

Allow yourself to be led by your higher power in this process. Be deeply devoted to your intentions. When you truly start saying yes to yourself, you begin to light up and therefore give others around you permission to do the same. This creates a ripple of *turning human beings into well-beings*.

Author Gabby Bernstein teaches how to co-create and manifest with the universe. Her book, *Super Attractor: Method for Manifesting a Life Beyond Your Wildest Dreams*, takes you on an empowering journey of co-creating with the energy of the Universe. Her teachings show you how to live a divinely guided life. To allow the flow of universal guidance, she teaches:

> *"The moment you embrace the wonder of Universal guidance, the more it will show up in your life. What you believe, you will perceive. Choose to focus on the guidance, intuition and direction that comes through.*
>
> *Feeling good aligns us with the Universe. This alignment offers us health, mental clarity, confidence, and reduced stress and anxiety. When we feel good, we are the opposite of resistant."* [55]

Whatever relationship you have to a power greater than you is supporting you in accessing your intentions. You are doing your part, and your higher power (whatever you believe in) is doing its part. Together, you are co-creating a life that will not only support your highest good, but supports the highest good of all of those who surround you.

What to Do When You're Stuck

You don't have as much time as you think. Life is short and

precious. Your time is your best and most precious resource — once it's gone, you don't get it back!

To be more intentional, constantly ask yourself: *Does this support the life I'm trying to create? Do my actions, thoughts, beliefs and energy match my intention? Am I letting life happen to me or am I living with intention?* Refuse to say you are "going" to do something over and over again and make a new decision right now.

A coach of mine once taught me a very powerful tool to help me move toward my intentions. She taught me to constantly ask myself: *What can I do right now, in this very moment, that will bring me closer to my vision?* Sometimes, the answer is to rest and take a break. Remember, you deserve to rest. When you prioritize your well-being, you can show up as your best self. Once you have that inspired download or idea, take action immediately — nothing is too small.

When you focus too much on the outcome, you forget about having fun along the way. Having fun during your journey is just as important as reaching your destination. Ask yourself this when you're stuck: *Is there another way to do this? How can I let this be fun like Friday night and easy like Sunday morning?*

Author and speaker Abraham-Hicks says:

> *"The reason you want every single thing that you want is because you think you will feel really good when you get there. But if you don't feel really good on your way there,*

you can't get there. You have to be satisfied with what is
while you're reaching for more."

Commit to the practices I've outlined in this chapter for building your intentions. Know yourself and what you want, have more fun, focus on feeling good, decide how you want to feel, and you will be well on your way to becoming a very intentional well-being!

A Summary of How to Unlock the Gold Key of Intention

- Utilize the five steps to setting powerful intentions to begin divinely designing your life: Get Quiet and Take Time to Think, Articulate and Define Your Intentions, Keep Your Intentions Alive, Release Your Intentions, and Co-Create Your Intentions with the Universe

- Resist the urge to focus on what you don't want, and instead put your attention on what you want to experience, feel, and have in your life.

- Commit to setting daily intentions with your morning practice. Know how you want to feel as you go about your day and what you want to accomplish beyond your to-do list.

- Release your attachments to your intentions and trust that you are being guided.

- Let yourself feel good now, and enjoy the journey of living intentionally.

Affirmations for the Gold Key of Intention

- I love myself. I am enough. I am worthy.

- I invest my time and energy where it feels right for me.

- I am powerful and I can create the change I want to see in my life.

- Everything I need comes to me at the perfect time.

- Life gets better and better.

- I know what I want, and I allow myself to receive it now.

- It's my time to shine and now is the perfect time.

- Happiness is a choice, and I choose it now.

- I am in charge of my own life, and I am in charge of my own feelings.

Turn Your Intentions into G.O.L.D.

Grab your journal and use these prompts to reflect on your next steps for unlocking this key:

G: What's **going well** with your intentions?

O: What **obstacles** are you facing when it comes to living intentionally?

_____

_____

_____

_____

L: What did you **learn** about intentional living from this chapter?

_____

_____

_____

_____

D: What do you intend to **do** next to be more intentional, based on what you learned?

_____

_____

_____

_____

You are powerful and you are creating your own reality. When you realize how safe it is for you to accept your own power, learn to trust your heart, and take actions that align with these beliefs, you will be unstoppable! I often refer to a quote from the famous poet William Ernest Henely to help me remember the role I play in my own life: "I am the master of my fate, I am the captain of my soul." Now, go live with intention!

CHAPTER 7

The Four Obstacles and a Path Forward

"Most people treat the present moment as if it were an obstacle that they need to overcome. Since the present moment is life itself, it is an insane way to live."
— Ekhart Tolle

"Every morning, when we wake up, we have twenty-four brand-new hours to live. What a precious gift! We have the capacity to live in a way that these twenty-four hours will bring peace, joy, and happiness to ourselves and others."
—Thich Nhat Hanh

This chapter came to me one day while I was meditating. I realized that I couldn't teach the solutions of unlocking the six keys without helping you to identify the current belief systems, thought patterns, and habits that are holding you back.

As you work to unlock the six gold keys to well-being, there are four common obstacles that may get in the way. I've seen these blocks show up time and time again in my coaching with countless clients over the years, so you are not alone if you struggle with any of them. It is very important that you address these obstacles to help you unlock the six keys to your personal well-being!

The reason so many people are confused about how to live a healthy life is because they're only focusing on the behavior. I can teach you all of the actions and behaviors to change in order to create health and happiness, but that's not what will create *lasting* change. The lasting change, and the part that most people miss, is the way you think, the emotions you feel, and the stories you tell.

You are powerful. Your mind is powerful. What you think about all day long becomes your reality. What you consume, what you watch, and who you surround yourself with becomes your energy. How you choose to see yourself, see the world, and view others is going to influence your level of health and happiness. *What are you thinking about?*

Albert Einstein famously said, "*There are two ways to live your life. One is as though nothing is a miracle. The other is as though everything is a miracle.*" How can you better allow yourself to choose to see as though everything is a miracle? It requires you to become a gentle observer of your thoughts, beliefs, and the stories you tell yourself.

I am going to break down the four main obstacles that I see as the most essential to overcome. As you explore these obstacles, please keep an open mind to the unlearning of what you've previously been taught. Change — *lasting, transformational* change — is possible.

Obstacle #1: Believing the Stories You Think

We all have negative, fear-based thoughts throughout the day. In fact, research has found that we think somewhere between 60,000–70,000 conscious thoughts per day, most of which are negative. And on top of that, the majority of those thoughts are the exact same ones as the day before! This means we are literally thinking the same self-limiting thoughts over and over, day after day.

Why do your thoughts matter so much? Because you will act and respond directly to the quality of your thoughts. The difference between people who are living a happy life and those who are living an unhappy life is that one group does not consistently *believe* these self-limiting thoughts. It's okay to be aware of your negative thoughts, but at all costs, you must avoid believing them.

Thoughts like:

- "I always have to be busy or productive"

- "I don't have the time to be healthy"

- "I'm too busy to cook"

- "I am not good enough to do that"

- "I could never have that kind of life"

— are all simply *stories* you are telling yourself. Even if the thoughts feel true to you right now, they are not ultimately true. They are only true if you choose to *believe* they are true. And if you believe these thoughts, your behavior will reflect them.

Neuroscientist and author Joe Dispenza explains more on this in his life-changing book, *You Are the Placebo: Making Your Mind Matter*:

> *"... we're addicted to our beliefs; we're addicted to the emotions of our past. We see our beliefs as truths, not ideas that we can change. If we have very strong beliefs about something, evidence to the contrary could be sitting right in front of us, but we may not see it because what we perceive is entirely different.*
>
> *We've in fact conditioned ourselves to believe all sorts of things that aren't necessarily true—and many of these things are having a negative impact on our health and happiness."*[56]

He continues on to say that we cannot create a new future by holding on to the emotions of the past. These negative thoughts are typically a response to an event that happened in the past — whether you experienced it directly yourself or the belief was passed on to you from your family.

What you think about all day becomes your life. Do you under-stand how vital this is? Your life is right now, and what you are thinking about dictates the lens through which you experience your life! If you're unsure whether you are thinking uplifting, positive thoughts on the regular, check in with your emotions. How you feel is a result of what you're thinking. Your emotions are simply guidance on whether you are thinking positive or negative thoughts.

I like to refer to the Abraham-Hicks Emotional Guidance Scale to check in with my emotions. The closer you feel to the lower numbers, the better you feel. The closer you feel to the higher numbers, the worse you feel. Listed below is the emotional guidance scale as described by Abraham-Hicks in Gabby Bernstein's book, *Super Attractor*:

THE EMOTIONAL GUIDANCE SCALE

1. Joy/Appreciation/Empowered/Freedom/Love

2. Passion

3. Enthusiasm/Eagerness/Happiness

4. Positive Expectation/Belief

5. Optimism

6. Hopefulness

7. Contentment

8. Boredom

9. Pessimism

10. Frustration/irritation/Impatience

11. Overwhelment (feeling overwhelmed)

12. Disappointment

13. Doubt

14. Worry

15. Blame

16. Discouragement

17. Anger

18. Revenge

19. Hatred/Rage

20. Jealously

21. Insecurity/Guilt/Unworthiness

22. Fear/Grief/Desperation/Despair/Powerlessness

Ask yourself what number on the scale you tend to live at. Where are the majority of your thoughts? What do you think about all day long? The goal with this scale is to simply think a better thought that will lead to a better feeling emotion. Notice what negative, self-limiting thoughts are on repeat in your mind...and then notice if your life is reflecting these thoughts. What kind of thoughts do you think the person who lives at the emotion of joy, empowered, and love has?

Learning how to stop believing self-limiting thoughts requires awareness and effort through contemplation and self-reflection. Changing your mind is not an easy task — you are working on shifting the unconscious to conscious and responding with your choice to change. As Darren Hardy, author of The Compound Effect, says, *"Picture where you are in [any] area, right now. Now picture where you want to be: richer, thinner, happier, you name it. The first step toward change is awareness. If you want to get from where you are to where you want to be, you have to start becoming aware of the choices that lead you away from your desired destination. Become very conscious of every choice you make today so you can begin to make smarter choices moving forward."*[57]

One of the best and fastest ways to move up the emotional guidance scale is to play the gratitude game I mentioned earlier in the key of mindfulness. The simplest way to describe the game is to focus on what you are grateful for. I challenge you to bring awareness to your thinking throughout the day, and when you are in a negative spiral of worry, stressed out over work, or feel anxious about a situation, play the gratitude game. Expressing your gratitude for all that is good in your life might sound like:

- I am grateful to my family.

- I am grateful for the healthy food in my kitchen.

- I am grateful for the sun shining outside.

- I am grateful for my warm bed and a safe place to sleep at night.

As you become aware of your thoughts throughout the day,

play the gratitude game and notice how you begin to move your emotions up the scale and feel better and better.

Simply reading this book is a huge step toward increasing your awareness levels, but creating the lasting changes you desire will require you to *apply* the knowledge and tools that you learn throughout this book. Not making the same choice as the day before is how you'll truly overcome this obstacle and improve your well-being.

Obstacle #2: Listening to the Noise

We are bombarded with noise all day long. Everywhere we turn, we encounter endless information, advertisements, and constant selling — everyone is trying to get our attention. And if we aren't careful, they will have it! Here are some examples of what I mean by "noise":

- The news and TV including videos, documentaries, articles, and websites that create fear and anxiety

- Gossip, listening to the negative opinions of others, listening to your negative opinions about yourself

- Scrolling and comparing on social media (ie: checking in on what someone else is or is not doing)

- Messy and low-energy environments (think: pictures on the wall that remind you of a time in your life that you would rather forget, or walking into a room that feels heavy to be around)

- Focusing on all the problems in the world rather than actionable solutions

- Doing anything that isn't in alignment with your own personal values

Our nervous systems weren't designed to know everything happening in the world. This doesn't mean that we should constantly avoid hard topics, but instead we can be more intentional by paying attention to one or two issues that truly mean the most to us and letting go of the rest.

Overcoming this obstacle requires you to live with intention, focus, and happiness rather than being in the noise. You have to be able to know what's important to you and turn everything else off, so to speak. This is your life we are talking about. You are only obligated to live your best life. Other people's opinions of what you should be doing and how you should be living are just that — noise.

You must become so self-aware and honest with yourself that you can identify when you are engaging in the noise, because we all do it from time to time. Your job is to identify the noise in your life and consciously **reduce** the amount of noise you allow in.

If you are not sure if there is noise in your life, bring awareness to how you are feeling throughout the day. Ask yourself often, "Is this thing making me feel good or bad?" Tune in with how you feel after engaging in conversations with certain people, attending an event, or watching a news segment.

Refuse to engage in the noise any longer! Take a stand and say *no more*. If you truly want the six keys to unlock better health and happiness, you need to create room to allow the new to come in. Have you ever noticed that when you are about to go through a change in life, you find yourself cleaning out your closet and other areas of your life? This is because you are clearing energetic space. Here are some ways to proactively create space for the new changes you are welcoming into your life:

- Turn off anything that broadcasts reasons to be afraid and depressed. This includes podcasts, news channels, music, youtube videos, radios, and certain pages on social media. If you feel afraid or have a pit in your stomach when you listen/read/watch it, that's your cue to turn it off and unfollow.

- Make your home a zen den complete with joy, peace, and love. Turn your home into a warm, inviting place full of things that uplift your energy. Remove anything that doesn't serve you or "spark joy" (also known as the KonMari Method).

- Stay away from people and communities who thrive on gossipping and pointing out what others are "doing wrong." Your circle should be inspiring, positive, and uplifting. Release from your life those who focus on problems and negativity.

- Let go of habits, behaviors, jobs, or activities that are not important to you. Every time you say yes to something, you are saying no to something else. Do not let that "no" be to yourself and what you desire to do.

- Reducing the noise in your life will help you have a clearer mind. And with a clearer mind, free of the excess negativity, you can choose to tune into better thoughts.

Obstacle #3: Having a Fixed Mindset

We are constantly living in between two minds: one is a mind that is closed and fixed; the other is open and always growing.

If we want to stay stuck in our patterns and behaviors, then we will live primarily through our fixed, closed mind. This is a mind that likes to avoid challenges and stay in its comfort zone. It prefers to stick to what it knows and avoids failure at all costs. It gives up easily when it's frustrated, and believes that it will always be where it is currently.

When I lived my life primarily through this mindset, I played small. I thought there was only one way to live — "the right way" — and that was to listen to societal norms. In this mind, I felt intimidated by others, jealous of others' success, and unworthy of having what I desired. I felt my opportunities were truly limited and that I would be living a certain life that others expected of me. I believed that my best years were behind me.

Notice how these thoughts bring up emotions of powerless-ness, doubt, and disappointment. On the Emotional Guidance

Scale, these emotions feel bad.

If we desire to grow and truly unlock a happier and healthier life, then we must live with an open mind. This is a mind that believes anything is possible. It chooses to see challenges and obstacles as opportunities to grow and learn. It is inspired by the successes of others and embraces uncertainty and trying new things. It believes that its current state does not mean that's where it will always be. This mind knows that literally *anything* is possible!

Notice how these thoughts make you feel the emotions of hope, optimism, joy and passion, which are emotions that feel good. The better your thoughts, the better you feel.

Today, I live my life through a growth mindset. I know that there are limitless ways to live, and that the "right" way is always what is in alignment with my truth — not what anyone or society says is the correct way. In this mind, I am inspired by others' successes, feel whole and complete with where I am, and I'm excited for where I am going. I welcome challenges as opportunities to grow and believe that the best is *always* yet to come.

Choosing to play big doesn't mean that I do it all myself. It means I ask for and accept support! We aren't meant to do it all — yet we think that we're supposed to. You are the most important asset that you can bring to the world. Let yourself be supported. Where can you ask for help? How can you allow yourself to receive the support others are offering you? What can you say no to?

Remember, these things will feel uncomfortable and will stretch you. Discomfort happens when you grow your mind to think bigger with all of the opportunities that are possible for you.

Mindset is the most important part of living a healthy lifestyle. Why do you see people who make it "look easy" — balancing a career, a home, a family, and still having time for self-care and vacations? Because they think differently. All of us have the ability to change our mindset to a different, more positive one. If you are stuck in a rut where you are struggling to find a healthy balance in your life, know that you are ready to do what it takes to create the lasting changes you desire. You are ready to sleep better, eat healthier, move more, spend time in nature, stay present, and live intentionally. *You are ready!*

Obstacle #4: Thinking Self-care is Selfish

Let me ask you this: do you feel guilty when you take time for yourself? That you "should" be cleaning the house, working, or spending more time with your kids? Do you find yourself ignoring your needs because you simply don't have the time? If so, you likely have the belief that it's selfish for you to take time for yourself.

Whenever you say yes to one thing, you are also saying no to another. For so many people, it's easy to say yes to everything around them except when it comes to themselves. You likely hate letting others down, but what about letting yourself down?

Self-care is the least selfish thing you can do. In fact, I believe it's more selfish for you to **not** take care of yourself! If you aren't taking the time you need to fill up your own cup (listen...this can be as little as five minutes a day), then you are constantly trying to pour into others from an empty cup.

You may have heard of this analogy before: you can't pour from an empty cup. While this is true, I want to challenge you to think even bigger — what if you only poured from an *overflowing* cup?

An overflowing cup means that you only give from the excess of energy and support that you have. What if you took such incredible care of yourself, let yourself be supported in every way, and had beautiful boundaries with friends, family, and work? What if you were able to give back purely from a state of overflow?

This is the core belief I want you to live from! Repeat this affirmation often: *Self-care is not selfish.* Choose to live from a state of overflow. This isn't just having your needs met and giving back from that — it's having your needs met and *then some*.

A Path Forward

It has been an absolute honor to guide you through this wellness journey! I am humbled and grateful that you chose to pick up this book and have followed through on reading to the end. My intention in writing this has been that you take exactly what you need from it to make the positive life long changes that you deeply deserve.

Now is your time to unlock your happiest and healthiest life. We all benefit when you are at your best — the ripple effect of you feeling, being, and acting your best goes beyond what you can possibly comprehend.

The relationship you have with yourself is the most important one you have in your life. This sets the foundation for everything else in life. It's important that you make time to meet your own needs. Cultivating a healthy relationship with yourself means practicing self-compassion and self-acceptance.

You might be wondering how you can fit in all of your well-being to-dos now that you've finished the book. You can do this simply by acknowledging what you need. Taking time to fit in your well-being to-dos doesn't mean that we neglect our responsibilities, our loved ones, or the world around us. It means that in all of life's beauty and distractions, we don't neglect ourselves. Take care of yourself, and remember to be your own best friend.

I believe in you! I know with every cell in my being that true health, happiness, and peace are not only possible — they are within your grasp. Trust yourself and the perfection of your journey. Transformation is a slow burn. This is not an overnight process. Go slowly but stay committed. Allow yourself to be truly transformed for life in this journey.

Congratulations on finishing this book! You should be really proud of yourself. I know that you are on your way to living a happier and healthier life and truly embodying well-being.

Remember: life can continue to get better and better.

Thank you for dedicating yourself to turning on your own light, so that you can be the lighthouse for those around you. I will leave you with one final quote that I want you to ponder, written by Paul Cohelo in his famous book *The Alchemist*, "... when we strive to become better than we are, everything around us becomes better, too." Shine bright, well-being.

Let's Keep in Touch.

A few ways to reach me:

- Subscribe to the Unlock Your Well-Being with Alisha Leytem podcast

- Email alisha@alishaleytem.com to inquire about speaking engagements, wellness coaching, or wellness workshops for your company or teams

- Sign up for updates of upcoming wellness retreats, workshops and other offerings at www.alishaleytem.com

Continue this conversation with me by sending an email to alisha@alishaleytem.com with "Work with The Six G.O.L.D. Keys to Well-Being" as the subject line, or learn more at www.alishaleytem.com

ACKNOWLEDGMENTS

First and foremost, I would like to thank my husband, Michael. Michael, you have been my biggest supporter and have believed in me more than anyone throughout this process. Your unwavering belief in me and my work is the greatest gift you could have ever given me. I love you so much. Thank you to Melrose, my beautiful daughter. Thank you for giving me the gift of becoming a mother and the opportunity to be the example of following your dreams — may this book show you to follow yours someday my sweet girl.

Thank you to my dear friends who helped me in the review of this book: Kim Leskovec, Kelli Baxter, Amanda Halabi, and Jess Morales. Words can't express my gratitude for all of you! Thank you to my incredibly talented designer, Caitlyn Alford — the key designs you created are so special! Thank you to my book cover designer, Austin Marshall. I appreciate your incredible work and support so much! Thank you to my parents, Russ and Kay Otting. You have always encouraged, deeply loved and believed in me! Thank you to my in-laws, Harley and Nancy Leytem. Your help and support is so appreciated. Thank you to my mentors and coaches over the years. Thank you for going first and showing me what's possible. I am so full of gratitude. Thank you, God! Thank you everyone!

The Six G.O.L.D. Keys to Well-Being Resources

To inquire about working with Alisha please visit:

www.alishaleytem.com

Assessment

The Six G.O.L.D. Keys to Well-Being Assessment

Take the *Six G.O.L.D. Keys to Well-Being Assessment*, a five-minute online questionnaire that will email you a report with your results. This report will give you an overview of your current level of health and well-being. You can take the free assessment at www.alishaleytem.com.

Book Resources

Download at www.alishaleytem.com

To access the resources discussed in this book (e.g. guided meditations, supplements, kitchen appliances list), please download them at our website.

Podcast

Unlock Your Well-Being with Alisha Leytem

This podcast is like attending a free weekly wellness coaching session. Alisha Leytem shares her love for mindfulness, wellness, and personal transformation in this podcast series.

Each episode is designed to inspire, educate, and awaken you to creating more health and happiness, and bring you one step closer to your best self. Available on iTunes, Spotify, Google Podcasts, and YouTube.

Professional Services

Wellness Workshops

With the state of the world changing at a rapid pace, organizations are needed now more than ever to provide strategic support for their employees physical, mental, and emotional health and well-being. We offer wellness workshops based on our Six G.O.L.D. Keys to Well-being framework, designed to help leaders better lead themselves so they can lead others better.

Coaching

We offer individual and group coaching opportunities that are customized to meet the client where they are at and support them in becoming healthier, happier, and more balanced leaders.

Speaking Engagements

Alisha's virtual or in-person speaking engagements are designed to inspire and plant seeds of well-being for lasting transformation.

Experiences

We provide experiences in nature that are designed to help

leaders reconnect with themselves, increase creativity, and create total mind-body well-being. From forest bathing experiences, to outdoor guided meditations, group hikes, and more — your team will walk away from this experience saying, "That was exactly what I needed."

Social Media

LinkedIn: https://www.linkedin.com/in/alishaleytem/

Instagram: https://instagram.com/alishaleytem

YouTube: https://youtube.com/alishaleytem

Facebook: https://facebook.com/alishaleytem

Notes

Introduction: The G.O.L.D. Method

1. Dispenza, Joe. *You Are the Placebo: Making Your Mind Matter*. Hay House, Incorporated, 2014.

2. Williamson, Marrianne as quoted in: Pasha, Riz. "101 Marianne Williamson Quotes That Will Enlighten You." *Succeed Feed*, 2 March 2021, https://succeedfeed.com/marianne-williamson-quotes/. Accessed 16 March 2022.

3. Hay, Louise. *Letters to Louise: The Answers Are Within You*. Hay House, 2011.

Chapter 1: The First Key: Sleep

4. "Better Sleep Habits May Help Reduce Heart Disease Risk and Aid in Weight Loss." *American Heart Association*, 3 March 2020, https://newsroom.heart.org/news/better-sleep-habits-may-help-reduce-heart-disease-risk-and-aid-in-weight-loss. Accessed 16 March 2022.

5. Williamson, A M, and A M Feyer. "Moderate Sleep Deprivation Produces Impairments in Cognitive and Motor Performance Equivalent to Legally Prescribed Levels of Alcohol Intoxication." *Occupational and Environmental Medicine* vol. 57,10 (2000): 649-55. doi:10.1136/oem.57.10.649, https://pubmed.ncbi.nlm.nih.gov/10984335/.

6. Häusler, Nadine, et al. "Association of Napping with Incident Cardiovascular Events in a Prospective Cohort Study." *Heart*, 2019; 105:1793-1798, https://pubmed.ncbi.nlm.nih.gov/31501230/.

7. Harvey, Allison G, and Suzanna Payne. "The Management of Unwanted Pre-sleep Thoughts in Insomnia: Distraction with Imagery Versus General Distraction." *Behaviour Research and Therapy* vol. 40,3 (2002): 267-77. doi:10.1016/s0005-7967(01)00012-2, https://pubmed.ncbi.nlm.nih.gov/11863237/.

8. "Wellness-Related Use of Common Complementary Health Approaches Among Adults: United States, 2012." *National Center for Complementary and Integrative Health*, https://nccih.nih.gov/research/statistics/NHIS/2012/wellness?nav=chat. Accessed 16 March 2022.

9. Link, M. R. S. "The 6 Best Bedtime Teas That Help You Sleep." *Healthline*, 14 Dec. 2021, https://www.healthline.com/nutrition/teas-that-help-you-sleep#1.-Chamomile.

10. Lynn, Anthony, et al. "Effect of a Tart Cherry Juice Supplement on Arterial Stiffness and Inflammation in Healthy Adults: a Randomized Controlled Trial." *Plant Foods for Human Nutrition, (Dordrecht, Netherlands)* vol. 69,2 (2014): 122-7, https://pubmed.ncbi.nlm.nih.gov/24570273/.

Chapter 2: The Second Key: Nutrition

11. "Close to Half of U.S. Population Projected to Have Obesity By 2030." *Harvard T.H. Chan School of Public Health*, 18 Dec. 2019, https://www.hsph.harvard. edu/news/press-releases/half-of-us-to-have-obesity-by-2030/. Accessed 16 March 2022.

12. Team, S. (2021, January 21). "Overweight and Obesity Statistics 2021." *Single Care,* https://www.singlecare. com/blog/news/obesity-statistics/

13. Michael, Pollan. *Food Rules*. Penguin, 2009.

14. Bauman, Ed. "Studies Show Microwaves Drastically Reduce Nutrients in Food." *GreenMedInfo*, 7 Sept. 2019, https://www.greenmedinfo.com/blog/studies-show-microwaves-drastically-reduce-nutrients-food. Accessed 16 March 2022.

15. Bara ski, Marcin, et al. "Higher Antioxidant and Lower Cadmium Concentrations and Lower Incidence of Pesticide Residues in Organically Grown Crops: A Systematic Literature Review and Meta-analyses." *The British Journal of Nutrition* vol. 112,5 (2014): 794-811. doi:10.1017/S0007114514001366, https://pubmed.ncbi. nlm.nih.gov/24968103/.

16. "EWG's 2021 Shopper's Guide to Pesticides in Produce | Dirty Dozen." *EWG*, https://www.ewg.org/foodnews/ dirty-dozen.php. Accessed 16 March 2022.

17. "EWG's 2021 Shopper's Guide to Pesticides in Produce | Clean Fifteen." *EWG*, https://www.ewg.org/foodnews/clean-fifteen.php. Accessed 16 March 2022.

18. Hosseinzadeh, Sahar Tahbaz, et al. "Psychological Disorders in Patients with Chronic Constipation." *Gastroenterology and hepatology from bed to bench* vol. 4,3 (2011): 159-63, https://pubmed.ncbi.nlm.nih.gov/24834176/.

19. Lewis, S J, and K W Heaton. "Stool Form Scale as a Useful Guide to Intestinal Transit Time." *Scandinavian Journal of Gastroenterology* vol. 32,9 (1997): 920-4. doi:10.3109/00365529709011203, https://pubmed.ncbi.nlm.nih.gov/9299672/.

20. "The More the Merrier. Why Diversity Matters for Your Gut Microbiome." *ZOE*, 25 August 2020, https://joinzoe.com/post/gut-bacteria-diversity. Accessed 16 March 2022.

21. Weston A. Price [@westonaprice]. Instagram, 17 June 2021. https://www.instagram.com/p/CQPU8Z_LwqP/?utm_source=ig_web_copy_link.

Chapter 3: The Third Key: Movement

22. Brown, Wendy, et al. "Prospective Study of Physical Activity and Depressive Symptoms in Middle-Aged Women." *American Journal of Preventive Medicine*. November 2005. https://www.ajpmonline.org/article/S0749-3797(05)00254-0/fulltext.

23. Laskowski, M.D., and R. Edward. "What are the Risks of Sitting Too Much?" *Mayo Clinic*, 2020, https://www.mayoclinic.org/healthy-lifestyle/adult-health/expert-answers/sitting/faq-20058005. Accessed 10 March 2022.

24. "Stanford Study Finds Walking Improves Creativity." *Stanford News*, 24 April 2014 https://news.stanford.edu/2014/04/24/walking-vs-sitting-042414/.

25. Thoreau, Henry David. *Journal*, 20 April 1840, https://www.walden.org/work/journal-i-1837-1846./

26. Chu, Paula, et al. "The Effectiveness of Yoga in Modifying Risk Factors for Cardiovascular Disease and Metabolic Syndrome." *Sage Journals*, https://journals.sagepub.com/doi/abs/10.1177/2047487314562741.

27. Volpi, Elena, et al. "Muscle Tissue Changes with Aging." *Current Opinion in Clinical Nutrition and Metabolic Care* vol. 7,4 (2004): 405-10. doi:10.1097/01.mco.0000134362.76653.b2, https://pubmed.ncbi.nlm.nih.gov/15192443/.

Chapter 4: The Fourth Key: Nature

28. Klepeis, N., et al. "The National Human Activity Pattern Survey (NHAPS): A Resource for Assessing Exposure to Environmental Pollutants." *Journal of Exposure Science & Environmental Epidemiology*, 11, 231–252 (2001). https://doi.org/10.1038/sj.jea.7500165.

29. Louv, Richard. *Last Child in the Woods*. Algonquin Books, 2008.

30. *John of the Mountains: The Unpublished Journals of John Muir*. (1938), page 320.

31. Twohig, Caoimhe. "It's Official--Spending Time Outside is Good for You." *ScienceDaily*, 6 July 2018, https://neuro-sciencenews.com/health-outside-9528/. Accessed 2 February 2022.

32. Anderson, Liisa, et al. "Nature Exposure and Its Effects on Immune System Functioning: A Systematic Review." *International Journal of Environmental Research and Public Health*, 2021 Feb; 18(4): 1416. Published online 3 Feb. 2021, https://www.ncbi.nlm.nih.gov/pmc/articles/PMC7913501/#.

33. Dass, Ram. "On Judging Yourself Less Harshly Ram Dass." *Ram Dass*, https://www.ramdass.org/judging-less-harshly/. Accessed 2 February 2022.

34. Mejia, Robin. "Green Exercise May Be Good for Your Head." *Environ. Sci. Technol.* 2010, 44, 10, 3649 Publication Date: April 21, 2010, https://pubs.acs.org/doi/10.1021/es101129n.

35. Oschman, James L., et al "The Effects of Grounding (Earthing) on Inflammation, the Immune Response, Wound Healing, and Prevention and Treatment of Chronic Inflammatory and Autoimmune Diseases,"

Journal of Inflammation Research 8, 24 March 2015: 83-96

Chevalier, G. "The Effect of Grounding the Human Body on Mood." *Psychological Reports.* 2015;116(2):534-542. doi:10.2466/06.PR0.116k21w5

36. Koniver, Laura. *The Earth Prescription: Discover the Healing Power of Nature with Grounding Practices for Every Season.* New Harbinger Publications, 2020.

37. Methorst, Joel, et al. "The Importance of Species Diversity for Human Well-being in Europe." *Ecological Economics*, Volume 181, 2021, 106917, ISSN 0921-8009, https://www.sciencedirect.com/science/article/pii/ S0921800920322084?via%3Dihub.

38. "Time for More Vitamin D." *Harvard Health*, 1 Sept. 2008, https://www.health.harvard.edu/staying-healthy/time-for-more-vitamin-d. Accessed 2 February 2022.

39. Li, Qing. *Forest Bathing: How Trees Can Help You Find Health and Happiness.* 17 April 2018

40. Li, Qing. "Effect of Forest Bathing Trips on Human Immune Function." *Environ Health Prev Med*, 15: 9–17. Published online 2009 Mar 25. https://doi.org/10.1007/ s12199-008-0068-3.

41. Goel, N, et al. "Controlled Trial of Bright Light and Negative Air Ions for Chronic Depression." *Psychol Med.* 2005 Jul;35(7):945-55. doi: 10.1017/s0033291705005027.